Ancient Masonic Lore

Elijah Abner

Ancient Masonic Lore

DEDICATION

This book is dedicated to the builders and safe keepers of the craft. May it bring light to your darkness, comfort to your troubled soul, and compassion to your weary heart while on your masonic journey.

Ancient Masonic Lore

CONTENTS

ix

Know Thyself

x

The Mason's Celestial Journey: A Tale of Hard Work and Divine Rewards

Once upon a time, there was a man named Joel. Joel was a master mason, a skilled builder of stone structures, who dedicated his life to serving others. He worked tirelessly, building houses of worship and public buildings that would serve his community for generations to come.

Despite the long hours and grueling labor, Joel never lost sight of the importance of his work. He saw himself as a servant of a higher power, and he knew that his creations would stand as a testament to his devotion and hard work.

As the years passed, Joel grew old and tired. He knew that his time on earth was coming to an end, but he also knew that his legacy would live on through the structures he had built. And so, with a heavy heart, he lay down his tools and closed his eyes for the final time.

To his surprise, when he opened his eyes again, he found himself in a strange and wondrous place. It was a place of light and beauty, where the very air seemed to shimmer with the presence of the divine.

Joel looked around in wonder, and as he did, he saw a figure approaching. It was the Great Architect of the Universe, come to meet him.

"Joel," said the architect, "You have served me well. Your life was one of hard work and selflessness, and I am proud of what you have accomplished. As a reward for your service, I would like to offer you a place in my kingdom."

Joel was overjoyed. He had never expected to receive such a reward, but he was grateful nonetheless. He knelt before the great architect and thanked him from the bottom of his heart.

And so, Joel became a resident of the celestial realm, where he continued to serve the Great Architect and his fellow beings. He spent his days exploring the beauty of the universe and building structures that would endure for eternity.

And every day, Joel was grateful for the life he had lived and the reward that he had received. He knew that he had truly lived a life of purpose and meaning, and that his hard work had been rewarded in the most incredible way imaginable.

The Stonecutter's Lesson: A Tale of Mercy and Understanding

Once upon a time, in a small village nestled in the hills of Galilee, there lived a young apprentice mason named Jacob. Jacob was a proud and haughty young man, quick to judge others and slow to show mercy. He believed that his skills as a mason were the only measure of a man's worth, and he looked down upon those who did not share his talent.

Despite his haughty attitude, Jacob was a talented mason, and he worked hard to hone his skills. He was constantly in demand for his work, building magnificent homes and temples for the wealthy and powerful. But despite his success, Jacob was never truly happy. He felt empty inside, as if something was missing from his life.

One day, as Jacob was walking through the village, he came across a stranger. The stranger was a poor and bedraggled man, with clothes that were torn and worn. He was begging for food and shelter, and Jacob sneered at him, saying, "What use are you to me? You have no skills, no worth. Be gone from my sight!"

But the stranger did not leave. Instead, he looked at Jacob with gentle eyes and said, "My son, do not judge me by my appearance, for there is much more to a man than his outward form. I have learned a valuable lesson in my travels, and I would share it with you, if you would listen."

Intrigued, Jacob asked the stranger what he meant. And so, the stranger began to tell a story.

"Once, there was a wise king who ruled over a great kingdom. This king had a magnificent palace, built of the finest stones and richest materials. The king was very proud of his palace, and he believed that it was a reflection of his own greatness.

One day, a traveler came to the kingdom and asked to see the palace. The king was pleased to show it off, and he led the traveler through each room, pointing out all of its grandeur. But when they came to the final room, the traveler stopped and looked around.

'This room is empty,' he said.

'Empty?' asked the king. 'What do you mean, empty? It is the finest room in the palace!'

'It may be the finest room,' said the traveler, 'but it is empty. For it has no love, no compassion, no mercy. And without these things, it is nothing more than a pile of stones.'

The king was struck by the traveler's words, and he realized that he had been judging people by their outward appearance, just as Jacob was doing. And so, he changed his ways, and became a just and merciful king, loved by all who knew him."

When the stranger finished his story, he looked at Jacob and said, "And so, my son, do not judge others by their appearance, for there is much more to a man than what meets the eye. Treat all people with kindness and mercy, and you will find that your own life will be filled with love and joy."

Jacob was deeply moved by the stranger's words, and he felt ashamed of his haughty attitude. He asked the stranger to forgive him, and offered him food and a place to stay. And from that day forward, Jacob lived a life of compassion and understanding, treating all people with kindness and respect.

As he helped the stranger, Jacob began to see that there was more to life than just his masonry skills. He discovered the joy of helping others, of making a difference in their lives. And he found that his own life was enriched by these acts of kindness and mercy.

Years went by, and Jacob became known throughout the village as a kind and compassionate man. People sought him out for advice and comfort, and he was loved by all who knew him. And although he was still proud of his masonry skills, he now saw them as a means of helping others, rather than as a measure of his own worth.

One day, a great disaster struck the village. A powerful earthquake had caused much damage, and many of the homes and temples had been destroyed. The people of the village were afraid and confused, not knowing what to do. But Jacob stepped forward, offering his services to help rebuild their homes and temples.

With his masonry skills, Jacob worked tirelessly to restore the village. But he also brought something even more valuable to the effort - his compassion and understanding. He listened to the people's fears and concerns, and offered comfort and hope. And as he worked, he taught others his valuable lesson about judging others and treating people right.

In the end, the village was restored to its former glory, and the people were filled with gratitude for Jacob and his efforts. And although he was no longer the haughty young man he once was, Jacob was now a true master mason, in the truest sense of the word.

And so, the story of the stonecutter's lesson is still remembered and retold, a testament to the power of compassion and understanding, and a reminder that there is much more to a person than what meets the eye.

The Mason's Test: A Tale of King Solomon's Temple

In the days of King Solomon, there was a mason named Hiral who was known for his skill and precision in the craft of building. He was chosen to work on the grandest project of his time, the construction of the Temple of King Solomon in Jerusalem.

One day, as Hiral was laying the foundation stones of the Temple, a mysterious being approached him and offered to reveal the secrets of the mason's craft. The being promised Hiral wealth and power beyond his wildest dreams, if only he would accept the offer and share the secrets with others.

At first, Hiral was tempted by the offer. The thought of having such wealth and power was too much to resist. But as he reached out to take the being's hand, a voice echoed in his mind, warning him of the danger of greed and the importance of upholding the values and morals of the craft.

Hiral paused, his hand hovering over the being's offered hand. He thought of the sacred responsibility he had been entrusted with, to build a Temple to honor the Lord. He thought of the pride he felt in his craft and the importance of preserving its secrets for future generations.

With a deep breath, Hiral made his decision. He withdrew his hand and turned away from the being, dedicating himself to upholding the values and morals of the mason's craft. The being disappeared, and Hiral never saw it again.

From that day forward, Hiral's reputation as a mason of great skill and integrity only grew. He continued to work on the Temple, and his contributions to its beauty and grandeur were unmatched. And as he worked, he passed on the secrets of the mason's craft to the next generation, always teaching them the importance of upholding the values and morals of their craft.

The Temple of King Solomon stands to this day, a testament to the skill and dedication of Hiral and all the masons who worked on it. And the story of "The Mason's Test" serves as a reminder of the dangers of greed and the importance of staying true to one's values and beliefs.

Journey of the Faithful Mason: Through Trials and Darkness to the Light of Hope

In the land of Canaan, there lived a mason named Tobiah. He was known throughout the land for his skill in building structures and his strong faith in the Lord. Tobiah lived a peaceful life, working hard to provide for his family and serving his community. But one day, he received a vision from the Great Architect, calling him to embark on a journey to a distant land.

Tobiah was filled with apprehension, as he had never traveled far from home. But he knew that the Great Architect would never lead him astray, and so he packed his belongings and set out on his journey.

As Tobiah traveled, he faced many trials and obstacles. The road was long and treacherous, and Tobiah often found himself in the midst of darkness, both physically and spiritually. He encountered bandits and wild beasts, and at times he felt as though he would never reach his destination.

But Tobiah never lost hope. He held fast to his faith, knowing that the Great Architect was with him, guiding him every step of the way. And through his trials and hardships, Tobiah learned a valuable lesson - that even in the darkest of moments, there is always hope and light to be found.

Finally, after many months of travel, Tobiah arrived at his destination. He was greeted by the people of the land, who were in need of his skills as a mason. Tobiah worked tirelessly, building structures and homes for the people. And as he worked, he felt a deep sense of fulfillment, knowing that he was serving the Great Architect and bringing hope and light to the people of the land.

And so, Tobiah lived out the rest of his days, serving the Great Architect and spreading hope wherever he went. He was remembered as a faithful mason, who faced adversity with courage and found light in the darkest of moments. And his legacy lived on, inspiring others to follow in his footsteps, and to always hold fast to the hope and light of the Great Architect.

The Apprentice's Journey: A Tale of Patience and Perseverance

In the land of Canaan, there lived a young man named Joel. Joel was an entered apprentice mason, eager to learn the ways of the craft and become a master mason. He worked tirelessly, day and night, determined to prove himself worthy of the title.

However, as time passed, Joel grew frustrated. Despite his best efforts, he found himself struggling to understand the complexities of masonry and was filled with doubt that he would ever reach his goal. The journey seemed endless, and he was tempted to give up hope.

One day, while working on a particularly challenging project, Joel's mentor approached him and said, "Joel, the path to mastery is a long and difficult one, but it is also a journey of great beauty. Do not be discouraged by the challenges you face. Instead, learn to appreciate the beauty of patience and the greatness of the reward of success."

Joel was struck by these words, and he knew that his mentor was right. He began to take his time with each project, focusing on the details and taking pride in the work he was doing. As he did, he began to see the beauty in the craft, and he found joy in the work itself.

As Joel continued on his journey, he grew stronger and more skilled with each passing day. He learned to appreciate the importance of taking his time and savoring the journey, rather than rushing to reach the end. And eventually, after much struggle and perseverance, Joel became a master mason, a true master of his craft.

And so, the young apprentice who had almost given up hope had become a shining example of the beauty of patience and the greatness of the reward of success. His story was told for generations to come, inspiring others to follow in his footsteps and never give up on their own journey towards mastery.

Joel's newfound appreciation for the craft of masonry spread far and wide. He became known throughout the land as a wise and skillful mason, one who had truly mastered the art of patience. Many young apprentices sought him out, eager to learn from his wisdom and experience.

And Joel was always happy to share his knowledge and inspire the next generation of masons. He taught them that the journey was just as important as the destination, that each step was a chance to learn, grow, and appreciate the beauty of the craft.

In time, Joel's name became synonymous with the ideals of patience and perseverance. He was remembered not just as a great mason, but as a true master of the craft, a shining example of what could be achieved with hard work, determination, and a willingness to take the time to appreciate the beauty in the journey.

And so, The Apprentice's Journey became a timeless story, passed down from generation to generation, inspiring young masons everywhere to follow in Joel's footsteps and never give up on their quest to become a master of their craft. The beauty of patience and the greatness of the reward of success would continue to be celebrated and remembered, always.

The Stones of Envy: A Journey from Jealousy to Appreciation

In the land of Canaan, there was a young apprentice mason named Gideon. Gideon was eager to learn the craft of building and constructing, but he struggled with one thing: jealousy. He was constantly comparing himself to the master masons, who were known for their incredible skills and beautiful work.

One day, Gideon was assigned to work on a project alongside one of the master masons, a man named Elijah. Gideon was envious of Elijah's skill and the ease with which he worked with the stones. He couldn't understand how Elijah was able to create such magnificent structures while he struggled with the simplest tasks.

As Gideon watched Elijah work, he began to see that there was much more to being a mason than just the physical work. He noticed that Elijah approached each stone with reverence, treating it as a sacred object. He saw that Elijah took the time to listen to the stone, to understand its qualities and strengths, and to work with it to create something truly beautiful.

Gideon realized that he had been wrong to be jealous of Elijah's work. He saw that each mason brought their own unique gifts and abilities to the craft, and that each stone was a part of a greater whole. He understood that true beauty came from working together and appreciating each other's contributions.

Gideon's newfound appreciation for Elijah's work and for the work of all the masons inspired him to work harder and to become a better mason himself. He learned that true success came not from competition, but from cooperation and appreciation.

Years passed, and Gideon became a master mason in his own right. He continued to build beautiful structures, but now he did so with a different mindset. He approached each stone with reverence and appreciated the work of his fellow masons. He was no longer driven by jealousy, but by a love for the craft and a desire to create something beautiful and enduring.

And so, Gideon's journey from jealousy to appreciation became a lesson for all who heard his story. It showed that true success comes not from competition, but from cooperation and appreciation. It showed that the beauty of life lies not in what we build alone, but in what we build together.

As Gideon grew older, he passed on his wisdom and teachings to the next generation of masons. He taught them to work together, to appreciate each other's strengths, and to listen to the stones. He showed them that the true beauty of the craft lay in the journey, not just in the finished product.

Gideon's legacy lived on, and the masons of Canaan continued to build beautiful structures that stood the test of time. People would come from far and wide to admire their work, and to learn from their teachings.

One day, Gideon was approached by a traveler who asked him what the secret to his success was. Gideon smiled and replied, "The secret to success is not in what we build alone, but in what we build together. It is in the appreciation we have for each other's strengths, and in the reverence we show for each stone.

For when we work together and listen to the stones, we can create something truly beautiful and enduring."

And so, Gideon's journey from jealousy to appreciation became a timeless story of inspiration, one that was passed down from generation to generation. It taught people to appreciate each other's strengths, to work together, and to create something beautiful that would endure for generations to come.

From Devastation to Renewal: The Jeasa Village Journey

Verse 1: When the Ga'aton river rose high, And the waters swept through the sky, The people of Jeasa Village felt the fear, For their homes and their lives were no longer here.

Chorus: But from the ashes of their despair, Came a renewal, a new air. From devastation to hope, The people of Jeasa learned to cope.

Verse 2: In the time of their greatest need, The master masons came with speed. With their knowledge and skill in hand, They built dams to withstand.

Chorus: And from the ashes of their despair, Came a renewal, a new air. From devastation to hope, The people of Jeasa learned to cope.

Verse 3: The masons worked day and night, With their tools shining in the light. And the people of Jeasa came to know, That together they could weather any blow.

Chorus: And from the ashes of their despair, Came a renewal, a new air. From devastation to hope, The people of Jeasa learned to cope.

Outro: And as the sun rose on a new day, The people of Jeasa looked to say, Thank you to the masons, who helped them see, That from their troubles, a new life could be.

The Journey of the Master Masons: Rebuilding Jappa's Legacy

Once upon a time, in the land of Jappa, there was a magnificent temple built to honor the gods. The temple was a testament to the skill and devotion of the people of Jappa, and it was renowned far and wide for its beauty and grandeur. The temple was a place of worship, a source of inspiration, and a symbol of hope for all who beheld it.

But as the years passed, the temple began to crumble and decay. Earthquakes shook the land, and storms battered the temple's walls. The people of Jappa watched in despair as their beloved temple fell into ruin, and they feared that their legacy would be lost forever.

It was then that a group of master masons stepped forward, declaring that they would take on the task of rebuilding the temple. They were descendants of the original masons who had crafted the temple, and they were determined to restore Jappa's legacy. The master masons were seasoned craftsmen, but they knew that the journey ahead would be long and difficult. Nevertheless, they set out with determination in their hearts and a deep faith in the gods.

The journey of the master masons was a tale of perseverance and determination. They faced many challenges along the way, from the harsh elements of nature to the skepticism of those who did not believe that the temple could be restored. The master masons encountered obstacles that would have discouraged lesser men, but they pushed on, relying on their faith and their skill to carry them forward.

With each stone they laid and each beam they erected, the master masons felt the blessings of the gods. They knew that their journey was not just about rebuilding a temple, but about restoring the hope and inspiration of their people. And as the temple began to take shape once again, the people of Jappa were filled with hope and inspiration. They saw the temple not just as a symbol of their faith, but as a testament to the power of perseverance and determination.

Years went by, and the journey of the master masons was finally complete. The temple was restored to its former glory, and it was even more magnificent than before. The people of Jappa came together to offer their thanks to the Great Architect and to celebrate the journey of the master masons. They told the tale of the master masons' journey to their children and to their children's children, and it became a source of inspiration for generations to come.

The temple of Jappa stood as a shining example of what can be achieved when the heart is filled with faith and the hands are guided by skill. And the story of the journey of the master masons became a testament to the power of perseverance and determination, reminding all who heard it that anything is possible if one has the will to make it so. And so, the people of Jappa continued to worship in the temple, filled with hope and inspiration, and they knew that the legacy of their forefathers would endure for all time.

Enoch the Stonecutter: A Tale of Faith and Determination in King Solomon's Kingdom

Enoch was a simple man who lived in the time of King Solomon. He was a stone cutter, working day in and day out in the scorching sun of the quarries, chipping away at massive blocks of stone to make them fit for the construction of the king's temple. Despite the harsh conditions, Enoch took pride in his work and saw it as a way to serve the Lord.

One day, as Enoch was toiling away, he heard a voice speaking to him. "Enoch," the voice said, "You have been faithful and determined in your work, and I am pleased with you. But I have a greater purpose for you."

Enoch was stunned. He had always known that the Great Architect had a plan for his life, but he never thought it would be something as significant as this. He asked the voice what it wanted of him, and the voice replied, "I want you to build a new city, one that will stand as a beacon of hope and light to the world. And I will be with you every step of the way."

Enoch was filled with a newfound energy and purpose. He left his work in the quarries and set out on a journey to find the land where the new city was to be built. It was a long and arduous journey, but Enoch never lost faith. He knew that the Great Architect was guiding him, and that gave him the strength to endure.

Finally, after many months, Enoch arrived at the site where the new city was to be built. He set to work immediately, laying the foundation, raising the walls, and putting up the roofs. And as he worked, he felt the presence of the Great Architect with him, guiding him and giving him strength.

Years passed, and the city grew and flourished. People came from all over to see the magnificent city that Enoch had built, and they marveled at the beauty and grace of the buildings and the gardens. And Enoch, who had once been a simple stone cutter, was now remembered as a great builder and a faithful servant of the Great Architect.

The story of Enoch the Stone cutter is a tale of faith and determination. It reminds us that no matter what our background or circumstances may be, if we are faithful to the Great Architect, He will guide us to do great things. And it shows us that with determination and hard work, anything is possible.

Krispo: a journey through grief and forgiveness

Once upon a time, there lived a master mason named Krispo. He was known for his skill and precision in the quarries and was greatly respected by his mason brothers.

One day, after being away from his village for three months, Krispo returned to find that his beloved wife had passed away. He was devastated and struggled to come to terms with her death. He felt that Great Architect had taken away his one true love and he was consumed by anger and bitterness.

But his mason brothers, who had known him for many years, were there to help him through his pain. They offered him comfort and support and helped him to understand that death was a natural part of life. They told him stories of how they had also lost loved ones, but through their own struggles and grief, they had learned to forgive and accept their loss.

Krispo was hesitant at first, but with the help of his brothers, he began to heal. He started to focus on the memories he had with his wife and was grateful for the time they had spent together. Slowly, he began to forgive the Great Architect for taking his wife, and he realized that she was no longer in pain, but was at peace.

With his newfound peace, Krispo was able to return to his work as a mason and use his skills to create beautiful structures that would stand the test of time. He remembered his wife every day and was grateful for the love and support of his mason brothers.

Krispo's journey through grief and forgiveness was not an easy one, but it was a necessary one. He learned that loss was a part of life, but with the help of others, he was able to heal and find peace. He became a better man, a better mason, and his story inspired others to do the same. The story of Krispo is passed down from generation to generation as masons set out to work and leave loved ones at home.

Boaz the Master Mason: Guardian of the Temple's Inner Sanctum

Once upon a time, in the land of Jerusalem, there was a man named Boaz. Boaz was a master mason, known throughout the land for his skill in constructing magnificent buildings. He was respected by all who knew him, for he was not only a talented craftsman, but also a kind and generous man who was always willing to lend a helping hand to those in need.

At the time of King Solomon's reign, Boaz was one of the many workers tasked with building the grand Temple of the Lord. Under the guidance of the great master Hiram Abiff he worked tirelessly, putting all his skill and passion into the building of the Temple.

As a master mason, Boaz was often sought after by young apprentices seeking guidance in their craft. When others were too busy to take the time to help them, Boaz was always there, showing them the ways of the mason's trade and teaching them the secrets of the building arts. In this way, Boaz gained the admiration and respect of all the workers on the Temple, and he became one of Hiram Abiff's most dedicated workers.

Tragically, Hiram Abiff was killed and upon his death King Solomon took Boaz into his confidence and made him the guardian of the inner sanctum of the Temple. This was a great honor, for the inner sanctum was the holiest part of the Temple, where the Ark of the Covenant was kept, and only the most trusted and skilled masons were allowed to enter.

Boaz accepted this responsibility with grace and dignity, and he devoted the rest of his life to serving the Great Architect and protecting the inner sanctum of the Temple. He was known as a wise and just guardian, always fair and always true to his word. He was loved and respected by all who knew him, and he will always be remembered as one of the great heroes of the building of King Solomon's Temple.

Benaiah: The Persistent Apprentice

In the land of Israel, there lived a young man named Benaiah. He was an apprentice mason, eager to learn the trade and become a master in his own right. However, his path was not an easy one. Despite his tireless effort and dedication, he was constantly met with disappointment and frustration.

Despite the many obstacles he faced, Benaiah never lost hope. He knew that he was meant to be a master mason, and he was determined to achieve his goal. Day after day, he worked tirelessly, honing his skills and learning all that he could from those around him.

Unfortunately, despite all of his hard work, Benaiah was not allowed to work on King Solomon's temple, the most prestigious project in all of Israel. This was a great disappointment to him, but still, he refused to give up. Instead, he continued to work on smaller projects, always striving to improve and gain new knowledge.

Years passed, and Benaiah's persistence paid off. He met other masons who saw his potential and took him under their wing, teaching him the secrets of their trade. Slowly but surely, he learned new techniques and honed his skills until he was finally ready to take on the mantle of a master mason.

And so it was that Benaiah achieved his dream. He was finally recognized as a master mason, and his work was highly sought after throughout the land. But even as he basked in his success, Benaiah never forgot the people who had helped him along the way. He always remained humble and grateful, and he never lost sight of the importance of hard work and determination.

And so the story of Benaiah the Persistent Apprentice has been passed down through the generations, inspiring all who hear it to never give up on their dreams, no matter how impossible they may seem. For Benaiah's perseverance and unwavering spirit proved that with hard work and determination, anything is possible.

From Despair to Abundance: The Story of Amnon and Jonah

In the village of Xaster, there lived a poor farmer named Amnon. He worked hard every day, tilling the soil and tending to his crops, but no matter how much he tried, his efforts were in vain. The land was dry and parched, and the crops withered and died in the scorching sun.

Amnon was filled with despair. He had lost all hope, and his heart was heavy with the burden of his failure. He wondered why God had forsaken him, and why he was cursed to suffer so greatly.

One day, as Amnon sat in his fields, he was approached by a stranger. The stranger was a master mason by the name of Jonah, and he offered to help Amnon. Amnon was suspicious, for he had never heard of a man so willing to help a stranger. He asked Jonah why he was so giving, and Jonah replied simply, "For the love of Great Architect."

Despite his initial reservations, Amnon accepted Jonah's offer. And Jonah worked tirelessly, using his skills to help Amnon. He taught Amnon how to conserve water and how to make the most of what little he had. And soon, Amnon's crops began to prosper. The fields were once again green, and the sun shone down upon a bounty of crops.

Amnon was filled with gratitude, and he thanked Jonah for his kindness. He asked Jonah how he could repay him, and Jonah simply replied, "By spreading the love of the Great Architect to others." And Amnon did just that, sharing his good fortune with those in need and spreading the message of Jonah's kindness.

From that day forward, Amnon was known as a man of great wealth and generosity. He had been lifted from despair to abundance, and he never forgot the kindness of Jonah and the love of Great Architect that had transformed his life. And so, the story of Amnon and Jonah was told for generations to come, as a testament to the power of love and the grace of the Great Architect.

Amasa's Inheritance:
From Abel's Hands to a Generous Heart

In the days of old, there lived a man named Abel, a master mason who was known throughout the land for his skill and expertise in building. He was a man of great wealth, but he was also a man of great charity. He was always willing to help those in need and give to those less fortunate.

Abel had a son named Amasa, who was still a young boy. Despite his youth, Amasa was already showing signs of his father's kind and generous spirit. He was fascinated by his father's work, watching with wide eyes as Abel created beautiful buildings from stone and mortar.

One day, as Amasa watched his father at work, Abel called him over and said, "My son, I am proud of the man you are becoming. You have a good heart, and I know that you will carry on my legacy of charity and kindness." Abel then handed Amasa a hammer and chisel, tools of the trade for a mason.

Amasa was overjoyed at the gift and immediately set to work, eager to learn all he could from his father. Under Abel's tutelage, Amasa grew in skill and knowledge, soon becoming a talented mason in his own right.

However, it was not just his father's masonry skills that Amasa was eager to emulate. He was deeply moved by Abel's generosity and the love he showed to others, and he made a vow to carry on this legacy in his own life.

As the years went by, Amasa became known throughout the

land as a man of great compassion and generosity. He used his skills as a mason to help those in need, always putting others before himself. He was a true reflection of his father's heart, and his legacy of kindness and charity lived on long after he was gone.

And so, the story of Amasa and Abel was passed down from generation to generation, inspiring others to follow in their footsteps and build a legacy of compassion, kindness, and generosity that would endure for all time.

Maacahan: Legacy of a Master Mason

In the land of stone and mortar, there lived a man named Maacahan. He was a master mason, known for his expertise in shaping the rough blocks of stone into magnificent structures that stood tall and proud.

Maacahan was not just a skilled craftsman, but also a wise teacher. He spent many years training apprentices, imparting to them his knowledge of the trade and his love for the craft. And he did not stop there. Maacahan also taught his apprentices to be upstanding members of the community, to always do what was right and to help those in need.

Years went by and Maacahan's apprentices grew in skill and reputation. They became master masons themselves, building great structures and creating a legacy that would endure for generations. But Maacahan was not done yet. He continued to work, toiling day and night in the quarries to extract the raw material for his craft.

One day, as he worked deep in the quarries, a cave-in occurred. Maacahan was buried alive, his life cut short in the pursuit of his craft. But his legacy lived on. His apprentices, now grown men with families of their own, continued to build and to teach. They carried on Maacahan's mission to make the world a better place, one stone at a time.

And so it was written, that Maacahan's life and work would be remembered forever. For he was a mason, but more than that, he was a teacher, a mentor, and a friend. And through his work, his wisdom, and his spirit, he left a lasting impact on the world.

From Poverty to Prosperity: The Inspiring Journey of Abraham in Xaster

Once upon a time, in the village of Xaster, there lived a poor man named Abraham. He was known throughout the village for his hard work and humble spirit, but despite his efforts, he lived in poverty and struggled to provide for his family.

One day, a master mason named Joel passed through Xaster on his way to the quarries in Jepah. Abraham was struck by the kindness and generosity of Joel, who was always willing to help others and share what he had.

As Abraham got to know Joel better, he was inspired by the mason's skills and dedication to his craft. He realized that he too could have a trade, and he made a bold decision to leave Xaster and follow Joel to Jepah, where he could learn to become a mason.

In Jepah, Abraham worked tirelessly under the tutelage of Joel, learning the intricacies of the craft and honing his skills. He proved himself to be a fast learner, and soon he was completing projects on his own.

Years passed, and Abraham became known throughout the land as a master mason in his own right. He returned to Xaster, where he built a home for his family and helped to improve the lives of his fellow villagers through his work.

Abraham's journey from poverty to prosperity was a testament to the power of hard work and determination, and to the generosity and kindness of others. His story inspired many others to pursue their dreams and find their own paths to success.

And so, in the spirit of Abraham's journey, let us be inspired to be masters of our own lives and to help others along the way. For in the end, it is not wealth or material possessions that define us, but the good we do and the lives we touch. Amen.

Aaron's Journey: From Apprentice to Master Mason

Once upon a time in the land of Israel, there lived a young man named Aaron. He was an apprentice mason, eager to hone his skills and become a master in his trade. His dream was to one day work on the grand temple of King Solomon, the most magnificent building in all the land.

So, with a heavy heart, Aaron bid farewell to his family and set out on his journey across the scorching deserts and rolling hills of Israel. His journey was long and treacherous, but he was determined to reach his goal.

One day, after many weeks of traveling, Aaron finally arrived in Jerusalem, the city where King Solomon's temple was being built. He was awestruck by the grandeur of the temple, its walls towering high into the sky and its gleaming pillars stretching towards the heavens.

Aaron approached the foreman of the construction site and asked for a job. The foreman was impressed by Aaron's determination and skill, and offered him a place among the masons. Aaron was overjoyed and threw himself into his work, eager to learn as much as he could from the master masons.

As the years passed, Aaron proved himself to be a diligent and talented mason. He worked tirelessly, never once losing sight of his goal of one day becoming a master mason. His skills grew with each passing day, and he soon became known among the other masons for his exceptional talent.

Finally, after many years of hard work and dedication, Aaron was approached by the foreman and offered the title of master mason. He was overjoyed and thanked the Great Architect for his blessings.

From that day forward, Aaron worked on many grand building projects, but he never forgot the temple of King Solomon and the journey that had brought him there. He was proud to have been a part of such a magnificent structure, built to honor the Great Architecd and serve as a symbol of His power and greatness.

And so, Aaron's journey came full circle, from a humble apprentice to a master mason, his name forever remembered as one of the greatest builders in the land of Israel.

Bearing Stones: A Story of Forgiveness and Restoration

Once upon a time, in the land of Canaan, there lived a master mason named Jacob. He was known throughout the land for his skill in shaping stone into beautiful structures, and was greatly respected by all who knew him.

One day, Jacob's younger brother Zeke came to him, seeking his help in building a great temple for the Great Architect. Jacob was overjoyed to work alongside his brother and eagerly agreed to help.

However, as they worked on the temple, Zeke became envious of Jacob's skill and success. He began to plot against him, spreading lies about Jacob to the other workers and ultimately betraying him by sabotaging the temple's foundations.

Jacob was devastated by his brother's treachery, and felt deeply hurt and betrayed. He confronted Zeke, demanding an explanation for his actions, but Zeke was unrepentant, and refused to apologize or make amends.

In the days that followed, Jacob struggled with feelings of anger and resentment towards his brother. He felt like giving up on the temple, and on his own life. But then, he remembered the teachings of the Great Architect and the importance of forgiveness.

With a heavy heart, Jacob went to Zeke and forgave him for his betrayal. He offered his hand in reconciliation, and to his surprise, Zeke tearfully accepted, vowing to make things right.

Together, Jacob and Zeke worked to restore the temple, using their combined skills to build it stronger and more beautiful than ever before. The Jacob smiled upon their efforts, and the temple became a symbol of their restored relationship and the power of forgiveness.

And so, Jacob and Zeke lived the rest of their lives as close brothers, bearing stones of love and forgiveness, and serving the Great Architect together. And their story became a testament to the power of redemption and the transformative nature of forgiveness.

A Builder's Heart: The Story of Daniel

In the land of Israel, there was a master mason named Daniel, who was known for his great skill in building houses. Daniel had a heart full of compassion and he felt a deep calling to help the poor and the homeless who lived in the land. So he journeyed across Israel, offering his services to those in need, building houses for the less fortunate.

One day, Daniel arrived in a small village, where he found that many of the people were homeless and lived in shoddy shelters. They had no one to help them build proper houses, and they were desperately in need of a home. So Daniel offered his services to the villagers, and they were overjoyed.

With the help of his apprentices, Daniel worked tirelessly, using his expertise to design and construct houses that were not only sturdy, but also beautiful. The villagers were amazed at the quality of the houses that Daniel built, and they were filled with gratitude for his kindness and generosity.

As word of Daniel's work spread, many more people in need began to seek him out. From one village to another, Daniel journeyed, building houses for the poor and the homeless, and spreading hope and joy wherever he went.

Years passed, and Daniel grew old. But his heart remained young, and his passion for building never faded. Despite his age, he continued to journey across Israel, building houses and bringing hope to those in need.

And so, the story of Daniel, the master mason with a builder's heart, became a legend in the land of Israel. For generations to come, people would remember his name and the great deeds that he had done, and they would be inspired to follow in his footsteps.

Solomon's Temple: The Elijah Chronicles

In the land of Israel, there lived a man named Elijah, a master mason, known for his exceptional skills in carving and shaping stone. Elijah was a man of great faith and lived a humble life, devoted to the Great Architect.

One day, King Solomon of Israel summoned Elijah and asked him to build a temple for the Great Architect, a place of worship like no other. The King was impressed by Elijah's reputation as the finest mason in all of Israel, and he knew that Elijah was the man for the job.

Elijah, who was honored to be chosen, accepted the task with great joy. He traveled far and wide, gathering the finest materials and the best craftsmen to help him in his work.

For many years, Elijah labored tirelessly, day and night, to build the temple. He was filled with the Great Architect's spirit and worked with such passion and dedication that his work became a true masterpiece. The temple was a sight to behold, with walls of solid stone and columns of gleaming gold, reflecting the light of the Great Architects glory.

As Elijah worked on the temple, he encountered many challenges. There were days when he felt discouraged, but he never lost faith. He remained steadfast in his commitment to the Great Architect and continued to work with all his might.

Finally, after many years of hard work, the temple was completed, and Elijah was filled with great joy and pride. King Solomon invited Elijah to come and see the finished temple, and Elijah was awed by the beauty and majesty of his work.

The temple became a symbol of hope and faith, a beacon of light in the land of Israel. Elijah's name became synonymous with the temple, and generations to come would remember him as the man who built a monument to the Great Architect's glory.

Elijah's story is a reminder to us all that with faith, hard work, and dedication, we too can accomplish great things. May we be inspired by Elijah's example and may the Great Architect bless our efforts as we strive to build a better world.

The Giving Stonecutter: Caleb's Legacy of Kindness

And it came to pass in the land of Canaan, that there lived a man named Caleb, a stonecutter by trade. Caleb was known throughout the land for his great strength, but more so for his kind heart. For he was always willing to lend a hand to those in need, no matter how great or small the task.

One day, a poor widow came to Caleb and asked for his help in building a new home for her and her children. Although he was a busy man, Caleb saw the love and concern in the woman's eyes and could not refuse her request. So he put aside his own work and devoted himself to helping the widow.

Days turned into weeks and weeks into months, and still Caleb worked tirelessly to help the widow and her family. And when the home was finally finished, the widow thanked Caleb with all her heart, saying, "You have been a true blessing to us. May the Great Architect reward you for your kindness."

And the Great Architect did reward Caleb, for his kindness and selflessness soon became known throughout the land. People came from far and wide to seek his help, and Caleb never turned them away. He used his great strength to build homes and shelters, to provide food and comfort to the poor and needy, and to spread joy wherever he went.

And so it came to pass that Caleb became known as "The Giving Stonecutter," a man of great compassion and generosity. And his legacy lived on, for generations to come told the tale of the kind-hearted stonecutter who always put others first.

And the Great Architect looked down upon Caleb and smiled, for He had created a man of great worth and purpose, a true servant of the people. And the Great Architect blessed Caleb, saying, "Well done, my good and faithful servant. Your kindness and selflessness shall be remembered for all time."

And Caleb continued to help others, spreading joy and hope wherever he went, always remembered as "The Giving Stonecutter: Caleb's Legacy of Kindness."

The Journey of the Master Stonecutter

In the days of King Solomon, there lived a man named Zechariah who was a skilled stonecutter. He had heard of the king's grand plans to build a temple to the Great Architect in Jerusalem, and he felt a deep longing to be a part of this project.

One day, Zechariah packed his belongings and set out on a journey to the holy city. It was a long and treacherous journey, but he was driven by his passion for the craft and his desire to serve the Great Architect.

When he finally arrived in Jerusalem, he found the city abuzz with excitement about the temple. King Solomon himself was overseeing the construction, and Zechariah was awestruck by the sheer scale of the project.

He approached the king and offered his services as a stonecutter. The king was impressed by Zechariah's skills and granted him a place among the team of builders.

Zechariah worked tirelessly day and night, cutting and shaping the stones with precision and care. He was inspired by the knowledge that he was building something that would stand the test of time and serve as a symbol of the Great Architect's presence.

As the temple took shape, Zechariah found himself filled with a sense of pride and fulfillment. He had left his home and family to pursue this dream, and now he was a part of something truly magnificent.

Years went by, and the temple was finally completed. King

Solomon dedicated it to the Great Architect with great ceremony, and the people of Israel rejoiced. Zechariah stood back and gazed upon his handiwork with tears in his eyes. He was filled with a sense of gratitude and awe at what he had been able to accomplish through his craft and his faith.

And so, the temple stood for generations, a testament to the power of human ingenuity and the grace of the Great Architect. And Zechariah's legacy lived on, remembered as one of the skilled stonecutters who helped build a home for the Great Architect in Jerusalem.

From Mourning to Mastery: A Stonecutter's Story

And it came to pass, in the days after the death of Hiram Abiff, the greatest stonecutter of the land, that a young man named Caleb was filled with grief. For Hiram was not only a master of his craft, but a mentor and friend to Caleb.

And Caleb said, "How shall I continue on without Hiram? For he was a light to me, showing me the ways of stone and the secrets of the craft."

And the Great Architect spoke to Caleb, saying, "Fear not, for I have not abandoned you. Look to Hiram's teachings and follow his ways, and you too shall become a master stonecutter."

And so Caleb took up the tools of Hiram, and he began to practice day and night, seeking to perfect his craft and honor the memory of his mentor.

And as time passed, Caleb's skills grew, and he became known throughout the land as a great stonecutter. And his works were a testament to the teachings of Hiram Abiff, and his love for the craft was evident in every stone he carved.

And the people said, "Surely Caleb has risen from mourning to mastery, and he is a fitting tribute to the legacy of Hiram Abiff."

And Caleb replied, "It is not I who deserves the credit, but rather the Great Architect who guided me and the teachings of Hiram who inspired me. For it is through their wisdom that I have become a master stonecutter."

And so Caleb continued to carve, using his talents to glorify the Great Architect and honor the memory of Hiram Abiff. And his story became a reminder to all that with hard work, dedication, and guidance from above, one can rise from mourning to mastery.

The Chronicles of Hiram Abiff, the Widow's Son: A Tale of Tragedy and Triumph in the Days of King Solomon

Once upon a time, in the days of King Solomon, there lived a young man named Hiram Abiff, the son of a widow. Hiram was known throughout the land for his exceptional skills as a master craftsman and builder. He was chosen to oversee the construction of King Solomon's temple, the greatest and most magnificent structure of its time.

Despite the many obstacles and challenges he faced, Hiram worked tirelessly to ensure that the temple was built to perfection. His unwavering determination and passion for his craft made him a beloved figure among the workers, and he was respected by all who knew him.

However, there were those who coveted Hiram's talents and sought to take advantage of his success. One day, while walking alone in the temple, Hiram was approached by three ruffians who demanded that he reveal the secret of his mastery. When Hiram refused to divulge his secrets, the ruffians grew angry and attacked him.

In the struggle that followed, Hiram was mortally wounded, and the three men fled the scene. The news of Hiram's death spread quickly, and King Solomon was deeply grieved by the loss of one of his greatest subjects.

Despite the tragedy of Hiram's death, his legacy lived on, for the workers were inspired by his determination and passion for his craft. They worked even harder to complete the temple in his honor, and when it was finally finished, it stood as a testament to Hiram's life and his contributions to the kingdom.

And so, the story of Hiram Abiff, the Widow's Son, lives on as a tale of tragedy and triumph, a reminder of the power of determination and the enduring legacy of those who have dedicated their lives to their craft.

The Stonecutters' Oath: A Tale of King Solomon's Temple and the stonecutters journey of enlightenment

Once upon a time, King Solomon of Israel had a vision to build a magnificent temple dedicated to the worship of the great architect of the universe. To bring his vision to life, King Solomon sought out the most skilled stonecutters in the land.

The stonecutters were a proud and hard-working group of men, who saw their work as a way to earn a living and provide for their families. However, as they began their work on the temple, they began to experience strange and mystical events that led them on a journey of enlightenment.

At first, the stonecutters were skeptical of these strange occurrences. They would hear whispers in the night, feel a strange energy in the air, and see apparitions of beings that were not of this world. They were afraid and unsure of what was happening to them.

But as they continued to work on the temple, they began to understand the true nature of their work. They realized that the temple was not just a physical structure, but a symbol of their connection to the Great Architect. They saw that their work was a means to connect with something greater than themselves and to unlock their full potential.

The stonecutters then took an oath to always put their faith in the divine architect and to use their work as a path to enlightenment. They dedicated themselves to learning about the great architect of the universe and the secrets of the temple.

As they worked, they became wiser and more enlightened. They learned the ancient teachings of the Great Architect and developed a deep understanding of the universe and its workings. They also developed a strong bond with each other, as they shared their experiences and insights.

Years passed and the temple was finally completed. It was a masterpiece of stone and wood, a testament to the stonecutters' unwavering devotion and their journey of enlightenment. People from all over the land came to marvel at the temple and to pay homage to the Great Architect of the Universe.

And so, the story of the stonecutters' oath has been passed down from generation to generation, serving as a reminder of the power of determination, devotion, and enlightenment. The temple still stands today, a symbol of the stonecutters' journey and a testament to the greatness of the Great Architect.

The Mercy of Hiram Abiff"

In the land of Canaan, there was a man named Hiram Abiff who was known for his skill in the construction trade and his unwavering faith in the Great Architect. One day, the Great Architect called upon Hiram to build a temple for His people, and Hiram accepted the task with joy and dedication.

However, there were those among the people who were envious of Hiram's success and the favor that he had received from the Great Architect. They plotted to kill him, so that they could take his place.

And so it came to pass that Hiram was slain in the very temple that he had labored so hard to build. But even in death, Hiram's spirit lived on, and he appeared to his killers in a vision.

"Why have you taken my life?" asked Hiram, his voice filled with sadness.

The killers hung their heads in shame, for they knew that they had acted wrongly. "We were envious of your success," they said, "and we wanted to take your place as the builders of the temple."

But to their amazement, Hiram did not condemn them or cast them away. Instead, he spoke to them of the Great Architect's mercy and love, and he forgave them for their transgression.

"The Great Architect is a God of mercy," said Hiram, "and He calls us to follow in His footsteps. Though you have sinned against me, I forgive you, for the sake of the Great Architect and for the sake of his temple."

And so it was that the killers were reconciled to Hiram and to the Great Architect. The temple that Hiram had labored so hard to build became a place of peace and reconciliation, a place where all who entered could find mercy and hope.

And thus it is written, that the spirit of Hiram Abiff shall forever be remembered as a shining example of the mercy of the Great Architect, and that his name shall be honored among the saints of the Great Architect for generations to come.

The Mason's Progression: A Story of Personal Growth and the Erection of King Solomon's Temple

In the land of Israel, there lived a young man named Jehoshaphat, a skilled stonecutter. He was known for his exceptional craftsmanship, but he felt that there was something missing in his life. He yearned for a greater purpose and a deeper sense of fulfillment.

One day, King Solomon called for the construction of a magnificent temple to be built in honor of the Great Architect. The king sought the finest builders and stonecutters from all corners of the land to work on this sacred project. Jehoshaphat, being one of the best, was among those chosen to work on the temple.

As Jehoshaphat worked tirelessly on the temple, he began to see the true meaning behind the project. The temple was not just a building, but a symbol of the Great Architect's presence among His people. The work he was doing was not just a job, but a service to the Great Architect.

Jehoshaphat's heart was filled with a new sense of purpose as he worked on the temple. He was determined to not only build a magnificent structure, but to also refine himself in the process. He spent time in prayer and meditation, seeking the Great Architect's guidance and wisdom.

As the temple neared completion, Jehoshaphat's skills as a stonecutter had improved significantly. He had a newfound understanding of his craft and a deeper appreciation for the beauty of creation. But most importantly, he had found a deeper connection to the Great Architect and a greater sense of fulfillment in his life. The temple was finally completed, and it was truly a masterpiece. King Solomon and the people of Israel marveled at the beauty of the structure, and Jehoshaphat was filled with a sense of pride and accomplishment.

The temple stood as a testament to the Great Architect's presence and a symbol of Jehoshaphat's personal growth and transformation. He knew that he had not only built a magnificent temple, but he had also built a better version of himself. And that was a true work of art.

The Chronicles of Shadrach: A Tale of Unwavering Faith

In the heart of Babylon, there lived a man named Shadrach. He was a faithful man, well known for his unwavering devotion to the Great Architect. Many were intrigued by Shadrach's steadfast beliefs, but many more were threatened by his refusal to bow down to their false gods.

One day, King Nebuchadnezzar issued a decree that all citizens must bow down and worship a golden statue he had erected in the center of the city. The statue was a symbol of the king's power and a demonstration of his control over the people. When Shadrach refused to comply, he was immediately arrested and brought before the king.

King Nebuchadnezzar was furious at Shadrach's refusal to bow down to the golden statue. He demanded that Shadrach be thrown into a fiery furnace to be burned alive as a warning to others who may dare to disobey. Despite the intense heat, Shadrach did not waver in his faith and was determined to remain true to his beliefs.

As Shadrach was thrown into the furnace, the people watched in awe as the flames rose higher and higher. The heat was unbearable, and everyone expected Shadrach to be burned alive. But to their amazement, they saw not one but four figures walking in the fire, including Shadrach, who was unharmed by the flames. The king, upon seeing this miraculous event, was struck with awe and declared that the Great Architect was real.

Shadrach emerged from the furnace unscathed and with a

strengthened faith. He became a symbol of hope for others, inspiring them to stand firm in their belief even in the face of persecution. The Chronicles of Shadrach spread throughout the kingdom, and his story became a testament to the power of faith and the unwavering devotion to the Great Architect.

From that day forward, Shadrach lived the rest of his life with a newfound sense of purpose, spreading the word of the Great Architect and sharing his story of unwavering faith. He traveled from town to town, preaching to anyone who would listen about the power of faith and the strength it can provide in times of trial. His story inspired countless individuals, and he was revered as a hero by many.

The Chronicles of Shadrach continue to inspire people to this day, reminding them that faith can conquer even the fiercest of flames and trials. It is a story of courage, hope, and unwavering devotion, and its legacy continues to live on, inspiring generations to come. Shadrach's name will forever be remembered as a symbol of faith and the strength it can provide in even the most trying of circumstances.

The Three Virtues: A Tale of Faith, Hope, and Charity

And it came to pass that in a village lived a man named Samuel, known for his steadfastness in the Great Architect and his unwavering faith, hope, and charity. And one year a great drought came upon the land, and the crops withered and the people were in want.

But Samuel did not despair, for he had faith in the Great Architect and hoped for a better tomorrow. And he took up the mantle of charity, going door to door and asking for any spare provisions to feed the hungry. And every day he cooked a hot meal and fed all who came to him.

And the word of Samuel's deeds spread far and wide, and many came to him for sustenance. Yet, he did not waver in his faith, hope, or charity, for he knew that the Great Architect would provide.

And so it came to pass that a group of travelers arrived in the village, bringing with them news of rain and provisions. And the rain came, and the crops flourished once more. And the people praised Samuel, calling him a hero for his unwavering faith, hope, and charity in the face of adversity.

And from that day forth, the story of Samuel and his Three Virtues was told and retold, inspiring all who heard it to have faith in the Great Architect, hope for the future, and show charity towards their fellow man.

And the Great Architect was pleased, for he saw that his

message of love and kindness had been spread, and the Three virtues of Faith, Hope, and Charity continued to live on, a testament to the enduring power of the Great Architect.

The Benevolent Builder: A Master Mason's Journey of Charity in the Footsteps of The Great Architect

In a small village on the outskirts of Jerusalem, there lived a master mason named Simon. Simon was known throughout the village for his skill in building beautiful homes, but he was also known for his kind heart and his love of the Great Architect.

One day, Simon felt a calling to do something more with his life. He remembered the teachings of the Great Architect and how He had instructed His followers to love one another and to help those in need.

Simon decided to use his skills as a mason to build homes for those who were less fortunate. He gathered together a group of other builders and they set to work.

As they worked, Simon would often stop to pray and to give thanks to the Great Architect for the opportunity to serve others. He would also take time to speak with the families who would be living in the homes, getting to know them and their needs.

Word of Simon's good deeds began to spread throughout the village, and soon people were coming from all over to see the beautiful homes that he had built. Some even began to follow in his footsteps, offering their own skills to help those in need.

But not everyone was happy with Simon's work. Some of the wealthy landowners in the area saw Simon's actions as a threat to their own power and influence. They feared that if Simon and his followers continued to give to the poor and needy, they would eventually lose control.

One day, a group of these landowners came to Simon and demanded that he stop building homes for the poor. They threatened him and his followers with violence if they did not comply.

Simon was not afraid, for he knew that he was doing the Great Architect's work. He stood tall and spoke with courage, telling the landowners that he would not stop building homes for those in need.

The landowners were furious and began to plot against Simon. They accused him of blasphemy and had him arrested.

Simon was brought before the Roman governor, who listened to the accusations of the landowners. But Simon did not falter. He told the governor about his work and how he was following in the footsteps of the Great Architect.

The governor was moved by Simon's words and saw that he was a good and honest man. He ordered Simon's release and gave him permission to continue building homes for those in need.

And so, Simon continued his work, never giving up on his mission to love and serve others. His legacy would live on for generations, inspiring others to follow in the footsteps of the Great Architect and to give generously to those who are less fortunate.

Hiram, the king of Tyre master planner and Builder

In the land of Tyre, there lived a great king named Hiram. Known for his wisdom, skill, and ability to plan and execute ambitious projects, Hiram was widely respected and admired by his people. He was also known for his love of the Great Architect and his unwavering devotion to serving him.

One day, King Hiram received a request from the great King Solomon of Israel. Solomon had a grand vision of building a magnificent temple to honor the Great Architect, but he lacked the resources and expertise to do so. He needed Hiram's help.

Hiram was delighted by the opportunity to serve the Great Architect and help his fellow king. He immediately set to work, gathering the best stonecutters, craftsmen, and builders from Tyre and its surrounding regions. He carefully selected each person based on their skill and expertise, ensuring that he had the best team possible to help him achieve his goal.

Hiram's team of workers was renowned for their skill and dedication. They worked tirelessly, day and night, carving intricate designs into the finest stones and assembling them with precision and care. Hiram oversaw every aspect of the project, ensuring that every detail was perfect and that the temple would be a fitting tribute to the Great Architect.

As the months passed, the temple began to take shape, rising up from the ground in all its glory. Hiram's team worked tirelessly, never tiring, never wavering in their devotion to the Great Architect and their commitment to their king's vision.

Finally, the temple was complete, a towering testament to the

Great Architect's greatness and to Hiram's skill and dedication. King Solomon was overjoyed, and he praised Hiram for his remarkable achievement.

In the years that followed, the temple became a center a beacon of hope for all those who sought the Great Architect. It was a tribute to the skill and devotion of Hiram, the Tyrian king and master planner and builder who had given his all to the service of the Great Architect's temple.

The Charitable Stonecutter: A Lesson in Giving and Entering that house not made of stone

Once upon a time, in a small village nestled at the foot of a great mountain, there lived a man named Simon. Simon was a stonecutter who had spent most of his life working with his hands, cutting and carving stones to build great structures. Despite his profession, Simon was a kind and generous man, who always made time to help those in need.

One day, while Simon was working in the quarry, he was struck by a falling stone and died on the spot. As his spirit rose up to heaven, Simon was greeted by the gates of that house not made of stones. However, the gates remained closed, and a voice boomed out, "Who are you, and what have you done to deserve entry into the kingdom of the Great Architect of the Universe?"

Simon replied, "I am Simon, a humble stonecutter. I have spent my life working with my hands and giving to those in need. I have provided stones to build houses for the poor, and I have given generously to those who had nothing."

The voice responded, "Very well, let me see what good works you have done." And with that, the gates slowly creaked open.

As Simon entered the kingdom of the Great Architect, he saw a beautiful city with streets paved with gold, and magnificent buildings of pure crystal. He saw people singing and dancing, and a great feast laid out before him. But what caught Simon's eye was the people.

There were people from every walk of life, the poor and the rich, the weak and the strong, all standing side by side, as equals. Simon noticed that many of them were people he had helped during his lifetime, and they greeted him warmly.

As he walked around the city, he realized that his charitable work on earth had earned him a place in the kingdom of the Great Architect. The people he had helped had not forgotten his kindness, and they had spoken on his behalf to the Great Architect.

Simon was filled with joy, for he realized that the true wealth of heaven was not in gold and crystal, but in the love and kindness shown by one person to another.

And so, Simon spent the rest of his days in that house not built of stones eternal up above, helping others and spreading the message of love and kindness to all who would listen. For he knew that it was not the wealth or possessions we accumulate in life that matter, but the love and charity we give to others that truly opens the gates.

The Stonecutter's Legacy: A Tale of Family and Forgiveness

In a small village nestled in the hills of Galilee, there lived a master stonecutter named Simon. Simon was a proud man, and he took great pride in his work. He had honed his craft over the years and had become known as the best stonecutter in the land. However, Simon's pride had blinded him to the needs of his family, and he had neglected them in his pursuit of greatness.

Simon had two sons, Levi and Ezra. Both of his sons had followed in their father's footsteps and had become skilled stonecutters themselves. However, Simon favored Levi above all others, for he had inherited his father's talent and ambition.

One day, Simon received a commission to build a magnificent temple on the outskirts of the village. He called upon his son Levi to help him with the task, and together they set to work. Simon was filled with pride as he watched his son carve the stones with such precision and skill. However, his heart was also filled with envy, for he could see that Levi was surpassing him in skill and talent.

As the temple neared completion, tragedy struck. Levi was killed in a terrible accident, leaving his father filled with regret and grief. Simon realized that his jealousy had caused him to neglect his family and had robbed him of the opportunity to tell his son how proud he was of him.

Years passed, and Simon grew old. He knew that he had one final task to complete before he left this world. He called his remaining son, Ezra, to his side and asked him to help him finish the temple. Together, they worked day and night, carving the stones with great care and precision.

As they worked, Simon told Ezra the story of his jealousy and regret. He begged his son for forgiveness, and Ezra, being a kind and compassionate man, forgave his father. Simon was filled with joy and relief, for he knew that he had made amends for his past mistakes.

When the temple was finally completed, the people of the village marveled at its beauty and grandeur. They praised Simon and Ezra for their skill and dedication. But for Simon, the greatest reward was the knowledge that he had finally repaired his broken relationship with his son and had left a legacy of forgiveness and family unity.

And so, Simon's story became a lesson for all who heard it. It reminded them of the importance of family, forgiveness, and the need to put aside jealousy and pride in the pursuit of greatness.

The Parable of the Stonecutter: A Story of Faith and Redemption

Once upon a time, there lived a skilled stonecutter named Shia. For many years, Shia had earned his living by carving stones into beautiful shapes for grand buildings, but one day, he was injured in an accident that left him unable to continue with his trade. Shia was devastated, feeling abandoned and hopeless as he thought that he had no other means of earning a living.

Every day, he prayed to the Great Architect to help him find a way to feed his family and himself. He wondered why the Great Architect had allowed such misfortune to befall him. He began to lose faith, believing that he had been forsaken by the Almighty.

One day, as he was sitting under a tree, Shia saw a man walking towards him. The man's face was radiant, and his clothes were unlike any Shia had ever seen before. The stranger approached Shia and asked him why he was so sad.

Shia shared his troubles with the stranger, explaining how his injury had left him without work, and he could no longer provide for his family. The stranger listened intently and then replied, "Shia, I am a messenger of the Great Architect, and I have come to remind you that your occupation as a stonecutter was only a trade. Your faith and hard work were what made you an exceptional stonecutter."

Shia was intrigued by the stranger's words and asked him what he meant. The stranger continued, "Shia, you have been blessed with great strength, determination, and creativity, which you used to excel in your work. Now, it is time for you to use these same qualities in other aspects of your life."

The stranger's words rang true in Shia's heart, and he felt a glimmer of hope. Shia realized that he had been too focused on his past trade and had forgotten that the Great Architect had given him many other talents. Shia began to apply his skills to other tasks and discovered that with determination and faith he could provide for himself and his family.

With time, Shia's faith in the Great Architect grew stronger, and he continued to work hard, embracing new challenges and opportunities. He found that he was not only able to provide for his family, but he was also able to help others in need.

Years passed, and Shia's life had changed dramatically. He no longer saw himself as a victim of his circumstances, but as a person who had been given a second chance. His unwavering faith in the Great Architect had led him to a life of purpose and meaning, and he was grateful for every blessing that came his way.

The parable of the stonecutter teaches us that our skills and talents are a gift from the Great Architect and that it is up to us to use them for the greater good. Even when faced with hardship, we should have faith that the Great Architect has a plan for us, and through hard work and determination, we can overcome any obstacle.

Divine Tools: A Tale of Faith and Redemption

In the ancient city of Jerusalem, there lived a group of master masons who were known for their skill in building the finest structures in the land. They were respected by all, and their reputation had spread far and wide.

One day, the group of master masons set out on a journey to a far-off land to work on building a grand new building. They packed their bags with all the tools they would need for the job, and set off on their journey.

However, on the way, they were ambushed by a group of robbers who stole all their tools and left them stranded on the side of the road. The master masons were devastated, for without their tools, they could not complete the job they had been hired to do.

Feeling ashamed and helpless, the group of master masons continued on their journey, hoping to find a solution to their predicament. They arrived in Jerusalem, where they were welcomed by the people, but they were too ashamed to admit that they had lost all their tools.

Days turned into weeks, and the master masons were still without their tools. They had lost hope and did not know what to do. But the Great Architect saw their plight and knew that they were great men who had been robbed of their livelihood.

One day, while the master masons were working on the site, a miracle happened. Suddenly, from the sky, a set of the finest tools descended upon the site. The master masons were amazed and filled with gratitude.

They realized that it was their faith in the Great Architect that had saved the day. They knew that it was only through their unwavering faith that the Great Architect had sent down the divine tools to help them complete their work.

With the divine tools in hand, the master masons set to work, and soon the grand new building was complete. The people of Jerusalem were amazed by the skill and craftsmanship of the master masons, and they praised the Great Architect for the miracle that had occurred.

The master masons, too, gave thanks to the Great Architect for the divine tools that had saved the day. They knew that without their faith in the Great Architect, they would never have been able to complete their work. And so, they returned to their homeland, filled with the knowledge that with the Great Architect's help, anything is possible.

Eliab the Faithful Mason

Eliab the Faithful Mason was a man who had been blessed with a gift for building. He had honed his craft over many years and was considered one of the best master masons in all the land. He had worked on many projects, but nothing compared to the grandeur and importance of King Solomon's Temple.

Eliab had been chosen to be one of the chief builders of the temple, and he was honored to have been given the opportunity to work on such an important project. At first, he was filled with enthusiasm and excitement. However, as the days and months passed, Eliab began to feel a sense of weariness and doubt. The work was hard and the hours were long, and there seemed to be no end in sight.

Despite his doubts and weariness, Eliab continued to work on the temple day after day. He knew that this project was important, not just for the kingdom, but also for his own faith. He prayed every day for strength and guidance, and he never lost faith that the Great Architect would see him through.

As the temple neared completion, Eliab was struck with a sense of awe and wonder. He had played a small part in building something that would stand as a tribute to the Great Architect for generations to come. The beauty and grandeur of the temple were a testament to the hard work and dedication of all those who had worked on it.

When the temple was finally finished, Eliab stood back and looked at it with pride and joy. He knew that he had been a part of something special, something that would last long after he was gone. And he knew that it was all thanks to his faith and trust in the Great Architect.

Eliab's story is a reminder that, no matter how difficult the task or how long the journey, faith and dedication can carry us through. It is a testament to the power of hard work and perseverance, and a reminder that, when we put our trust in the Great Architect we can achieve great things.

The Parable of the Apprentice Mason: Trusting in Yourself Through Faith

Once upon a time in Israel, there was an apprentice mason named Jacob. Jacob was very skilled in his craft and was always eager to learn more from his master. However, Jacob was plagued by self-doubt and worry. He would often overthink his work and become anxious about making mistakes.

One day, Jacob's master tasked him with building a new wall for a local temple. Jacob was excited about the opportunity, but as he started his work, he became overwhelmed with worry. He wondered if he was skilled enough to complete the task and if he would be able to create a wall that was strong and durable.

Jacob spent long hours working on the wall, but he couldn't shake off his worries. He was so consumed by his self-doubt that he even started to make more mistakes. The more he worried, the worse his work became.

One day, as Jacob was working on the wall, he met a man who had been watching him for some time. The man asked Jacob why he was so worried. Jacob explained that he was afraid of making mistakes and not being good enough. The man listened patiently and then told Jacob a parable.

"There was once a man named Daniel who had to cross a river. He was afraid to do so and worried that he would drown. As he stood by the riverbank, he met a wise old man who asked him why he was so worried. Daniel replied, 'I don't know how to swim, and I'm afraid of drowning.' The wise old man said to him, 'Have faith in yourself. Take a deep breath, step into the water, and you will find that its depth will only go up to your knees.'"

Jacob thought about the parable and realized that he was like the man in the story. He had the skills to build the wall, but he was too worried to trust himself. Jacob took a deep breath and started to work on the wall again. He focused on his skills and worked with a sense of purpose. As he worked, his worries faded away.

In time, Jacob completed the wall, and it was strong and beautiful. His master was pleased with his work and praised him for his skill and dedication. Jacob realized that by having faith in himself and trusting his abilities, he could accomplish great things.

From that day on, Jacob stopped overthinking and worrying. He had faith in himself and his abilities. Jacob became a skilled and respected mason, known for his work across the land. And he never forgot the parable of the wise man who had taught him the importance of not overthinking and having faith in himself.

Eli of Xaster: The Sacrifice of Childhood

Eli was a boy who lived in the small village of Xaster in Israel. He was just a child when his father passed away, leaving his mother to raise him and his younger siblings alone. Eli's father had been the primary breadwinner of the family, and his death left them struggling to make ends meet.

Eli was forced to grow up quickly, taking on responsibilities far beyond his years. He became the man of the house, helping his mother with household chores, looking after his siblings, and working in the fields to provide for his family. He never complained, knowing that his hard work was necessary to ensure that his family could survive.

Eli's life was filled with hard work and sacrifice. While other children his age played and had fun, he spent his days tending to the crops and helping his mother with the endless household chores. He missed out on his childhood, but he never regretted the sacrifices he made for his family.

As Eli grew older, his responsibilities increased. He was determined to ensure that his siblings had a better life than he did, and he worked tirelessly to provide for them. He was known throughout the village for his kind heart and willingness to help anyone in need.

Despite the hardships he faced, Eli never lost his faith in the Great Architect. He prayed every day for his family's well-being, and he believed that if he worked hard enough, the Great Architect would provide for them.

Years passed, and Eli's siblings grew up and moved on to start their own families. Eli remained in the village, still working hard to provide for his mother and himself. He continued to be a pillar of strength in the community, always willing to lend a helping hand.

Then, one day, disaster struck. A terrible drought hit the village, and the crops began to wither and die. The villagers were in despair, knowing that without a successful harvest, they would not have enough food to last through the winter.

Eli knew that he had to act quickly. He prayed harder than ever before and searched the village for any solution to the drought. As he wandered through the hills one day, he stumbled upon a hidden well, deep in the rocks. The well was still full of water, and Eli knew that it could save the village.

With the help of his fellow villagers, Eli dug a channel to bring the water back to the village. It was a grueling task, but Eli worked tirelessly, day and night, until the channel was complete. The villagers were amazed by Eli's determination and strength, and they all lent a hand in the effort.

Thanks to Eli's hard work and determination, the village was able to survive the drought. The crops flourished, and the villagers had enough food to last through the winter. Eli's sacrifice of his childhood had paid off in the end, and his family and the villagers were forever grateful for his help.

Years later, as an old man, Eli would often sit outside his home and tell the story of the drought and how he had found the hidden well. The children of the village would gather around him and listen in awe at the tale of the young boy who had sacrificed his childhood to save his family and his village.

And they would look up to Eli with admiration and respect, knowing that he was a true hero of Xaster. Eli's life had been one of hard work and sacrifice, but it had also been a life of love and faith. He had dedicated himself to his family and his community, and in the end, his efforts had paid off. Eli had proven that even in the darkest of times, there is always hope, as long as there are those willing to work hard and never give up.

Tyriah's Trials: A Tale of Faith and Fortitude

Once upon a time, in a land ruled by kings and prophets, there lived a young boy named Tyriah. Tyriah was a devout follower of the Great Architect of the Universe, raised by his parents to believe in the power of faith and the strength of prayer.

One day, disaster struck Tyriah's village. A great famine ravaged the land, leaving many families without food or shelter. Tyriah's family was no exception, and they struggled to survive in the face of hunger and despair.

Despite the challenges he faced, Tyriah refused to lose faith in the Great Architect. Every day, he prayed for strength and guidance, believing that the Great Architect would see him and his family through their struggles.

As the famine continued, Tyriah's faith was put to the test in new and challenging ways. He watched as his friends and neighbors turned to greed and selfishness, hoarding what little food remained for themselves. He saw families torn apart by hunger and desperation, and he began to question whether the Great Architect truly cared for his people.

Yet even in the darkest of times, Tyriah refused to give up hope. He continued to pray for guidance, trusting that the Great Architect would show him a way through the trials that lay ahead.

One day, as Tyriah was out gathering firewood, he stumbled upon a hidden garden. In the center of the garden stood a tree unlike any he had ever seen before. The tree was heavy with loads of fruit, and Tyriah then knew that it was a direct sign from the Great Architect himself.

He took some of the fruit back to his family, and they were able to survive for a few more days. But when the fruit ran out, Tyriah knew that he had to return to the garden and find a way to sustain his family.

For weeks, Tyriah snuck into the garden under cover of darkness, gathering fruit and vegetables to bring back to his family. Each time he went, he prayed for forgiveness, knowing that he was breaking the law by taking what did not belong to him.

Finally, one night, Tyriah was caught by the owner of the garden. The man was furious and threatened to have him arrested. But Tyriah stood firm, telling the man that he had only taken what he needed to survive, and that the Great Architect had led him to the garden in his time of need.

To his surprise, the man softened and listened to Tyriah's story. He was moved by the boy's faith and courage, and he realized that he had been hoarding his blessings instead of sharing them with those in need but reminded the boy of the importance of asking before taking.

In the end, the man gave Tyriah permission to take as much fruit as he needed, and he even helped him to build a shelter in the garden where he and his family could stay safe and fed during the famine.

Tyriah's trials had tested his faith and his fortitude, but he had emerged stronger for having faced them. He knew that the Great Architect had been with him every step of the way,

The Redemption of Makiah: A Tale of Envy, Tragedy, and Forgiveness

In the ancient land of Canaan, there lived a man named Makiah who was known throughout the village for his bitter heart and unrelenting envy. He lived a life consumed with jealousy and resentment, always comparing himself to his neighbors and feeling inferior to their success.

Makiah's greatest source of envy was his neighbor Lial. Lial had a prosperous garden and a happy family, which only fueled Makiah's jealousy even more. Makiah constantly fought with Lial, spreading rumors and lies about him in an attempt to bring him down.

Despite Makiah's best efforts, Lial continued to thrive, and his garden flourished year after year. Makiah's envy only grew more intense, and he became consumed with bitterness and resentment. He spent his days plotting ways to sabotage Lial's success, convinced that he deserved to be the one in Lial's place.

But one day, tragedy struck. Lial was working in the quarries when a terrible accident occurred, and he was killed instantly. His wife was left alone to care for their young children, and the entire village mourned the loss of such a kind and beloved man.

Makiah was shocked and devastated by Lial's death. He realized with sudden clarity how much time he had wasted fighting with Lial and being consumed with jealousy. He knew he had to make things right, to find a way to redeem himself for all the pain he had caused.

Makiah went to Lial's family and offered his help and support. He apologized for all the hurt he had caused over the years, and he promised to do everything in his power to help Lial's family in their time of need.

At first, Lial's family was hesitant to accept Makiah's help. They had seen firsthand the pain he had caused and were understandably wary of his sudden change of heart. But as time went on, Makiah proved himself to be a true friend and ally to Lial's family.

He spent countless hours in Lial's garden, tending to the crops and ensuring that they flourished just as they had when Lial was alive. He also took on the role of mentor and friend to Lial's children, teaching them the ways of the land and sharing stories of their father's life.

Through his acts of kindness and selflessness, Makiah was able to find true redemption for his past mistakes. He learned the power of forgiveness and the importance of seeking redemption for one's past actions.

In the end, Makiah's story became a testament to the human capacity for change and growth. He was able to transform from a bitter and jealous man into a true friend and ally to Lial's family, proving that even the most flawed among us can find redemption and forgiveness in the eyes of others.

The Piia Village: Rebuilding Hope Through Unity

In the land of Israel, there was a small village called Piia. The people of Piia were hardworking and honest, and they took pride in their community. They had built their homes and their livelihoods from the ground up, and they cherished the land that sustained them.

One day, disaster struck. A careless traveler passing through the village accidentally started a fire, and before long, the flames had consumed nearly everything in their path. Homes, crops, and animals were destroyed, and the people of Piia were left with nothing but the ashes of their former lives.

At first, the villagers were devastated. They wept and mourned, feeling lost and helpless. They wondered how they could ever rebuild what had been lost, how they could ever find the strength to carry on.

But then, something miraculous happened. They began to look around and realize that they weren't alone. Their neighbors were still there, and together, they had the strength to rebuild what they had lost.

So they set to work. One by one, they began to rebuild their homes, using whatever materials they could find. They worked tirelessly, day and night, until slowly but surely, Piia began to rise from the ashes.

As they worked, the people of Piia grew closer together. They shared what little food and resources they had, and they leaned on each other for support. They prayed together and sang songs of hope and resilience. And eventually, their efforts paid off.

Years later, Piia was once again a thriving community, stronger and more united than ever before. The people of the village looked back on the fire as a turning point, a moment when they learned that they could overcome anything as long as they worked together.

They had rebuilt their homes, but they had also rebuilt their bonds of friendship and trust. They knew that they could always count on each other, no matter what challenges lay ahead. And so, they took care to cherish their community, to protect it and nurture it, to make sure that it would be there for generations to come.

The story of Piia became a legend throughout the land, a symbol of the power of resilience and unity in the face of adversity. And the people of Piia themselves, they knew that they had been blessed by the fire that had nearly destroyed them. For it was through that fire that they had discovered the true strength of their village, and the unbreakable bonds that held them together.

The Tale of Jeriah's Journey to Honor His Parents and Care for the Elderly

Once upon a time, in the ancient land of Israel, there lived a young boy named Jeriah. He grew up in a small village with his parents, who were hardworking but struggled to make ends meet. Jeriah often saw his parents working tirelessly to provide for their family, and he knew that when he grew up, he wanted to do something to help them.

As Jeriah grew older, he developed a keen interest in the art of masonry. He loved the idea of building structures that would stand the test of time and be admired by generations to come. He began to work as an apprentice to a master mason and learned everything he could about the craft.

Jeriah had a natural talent for masonry, and his skills quickly began to grow. He worked on countless projects, from building grand temples to humble homes. Everywhere he went, he put his heart and soul into his work, making sure that every stone was perfectly placed and every structure was built to last.

But all the while, he kept his promise to himself that he would return home one day and take care of his parents. He knew that they were growing older, and he wanted to repay them for all the love and support they had given him over the years.

Years passed, and Jeriah finally returned to his village. But to his great sorrow, he discovered that his parents had passed away while he was away. He was heartbroken, but he knew that he could still fulfill his promise by helping the elderly in his village.

Jeriah dedicated himself to this task, visiting the homes of the elderly, offering his services as a mason to make repairs and improvements, and simply spending time with them to brighten their day. He quickly became known as a kind and compassionate person, someone who always had a smile on his face and a helping hand to offer.

Word of his kindness spread, and soon, people all over the village were following in his footsteps. They began to volunteer their time and skills to help the elderly, just as Jeriah had done. The village decided to honor Jeriah's dedication by declaring September 12th as a day to help the elderly. On this day, people from all over the village would come together to assist the elderly, just as Jeriah had done.

The day became known as "The Master Mason's Promise," in honor of Jeriah's commitment to caring for his parents and helping the elderly. It was a day of joy and celebration, as people of all ages and backgrounds came together to lend a helping hand.

As the years went by, the tradition of "The Master Mason's Promise" continued to grow. People began to come from all over the region to take part in the festivities, which included music, dancing, and, of course, helping the elderly. Jeriah was remembered as a kind and generous soul who had dedicated his life to helping others, and his legacy lived on through the annual celebration of "The Master Mason's Promise."

Jeriah passed away many years later, but his memory continued to inspire people for generations to come. His commitment to helping the elderly and his dedication to his craft had left an indelible mark on the village and on the hearts of all who had known him. And so, the tale of Jeriah's journey to honor his parents and care for the elderly became a legend, inspiring people to live their lives with kindness, compassion, and a commitment to making the world a better place.

The Book of Abraham: A Journey of Selfishness and Redemption

In the ancient land of Ur, there lived a man named Abraham. From a young age, Abraham was fascinated by the grand structures that adorned the city, and he dreamed of becoming a mason and traveling across the land to work on these amazing projects.

Abraham was the son of a wealthy merchant and grew up in a comfortable lifestyle. Despite the wealth and comfort he enjoyed, Abraham was always restless and yearned for something more than just material possessions. He found the grand architecture of the city awe-inspiring and believed that by becoming a skilled mason, he could leave a lasting legacy and make a name for himself.

As he grew older, Abraham became more and more consumed by his desire to achieve his dream of becoming a great mason. He worked tirelessly to learn the craft, spending long hours studying the techniques and practices of the best masons in the land.

However, as Abraham's skills grew, so did his ego. He began to see himself as superior to others and felt entitled to success and recognition. He started to cut corners and take shortcuts, believing that his natural talent was enough to carry him through.

As a result, his work became shoddy and dangerous, and people began to avoid him. His once-promising career began to falter, and he became increasingly bitter and resentful.

Despite his reputation, Abraham continued to dream of traveling the land and working on the greatest structures. One day, he heard about a magnificent temple being built in a nearby city and knew that this was his chance to prove his worth.

He set out to the city, eager to impress the builders with his skills. But when he arrived, he found that the builders were already well-staffed, and there was no need for his help.

Enraged, Abraham lashed out at the builders, accusing them of being jealous of his talent and trying to keep him from his dream. But as he ranted and raved, he realized the truth: he had been too focused on himself and his own desires to see the needs of others.

Filled with shame and regret, Abraham left the city and wandered the land. For years, he traveled from town to town, seeking redemption for his selfishness and trying to make amends for the harm he had caused.

As he journeyed, Abraham encountered many people in need of help. He saw villages destroyed by war, families struggling to survive, and communities ravaged by disease. With each encounter, he felt a deep sense of compassion and empathy for those he met.

One day, he came upon a small village that had been devastated by a terrible storm. The buildings were in ruins, and the people were desperate for help.

Without a second thought, Abraham set to work. He used his skills as a mason to rebuild the homes and buildings, and he worked tirelessly to help the people of the village. As he worked, he felt a sense of purpose and fulfillment that he had never felt before.

Word of Abraham's selfless deeds spread throughout the land, and people began to seek him out for his help and guidance. He became known as a wise and generous man, respected and admired by all who knew him.

In the end, Abraham realized that his dream of becoming a great mason had been misguided. True greatness, he realized, came not from personal achievement but from serving others and making a positive impact on the world around him.

He continued to travel the land, helping those in need and spreading love and kindness wherever he went. He lived a long and fruitful life, beloved by all who knew him.

When Abraham passed away, he was remembered not just for his skill as a mason, but also for the compassion and generosity he showed to others.

The Masons' Journey: A Tale of Friendship and Redemption

In the land of Canaan, there were two master masons named Hiram and Solomon. They were known throughout the land for their skill in building great structures that lasted for ages. One day, they received a call to work on a magnificent temple in a distant city. The temple was to be built as a place of worship for the people of the city, and it was going to be a grand project that would take months to complete. Hiram and Solomon were excited about the project, as it was a great opportunity for them to showcase their skills and create something truly magnificent.

Excited about the project, they set out on a month-long journey through the scorching desert. As they journeyed through the hot and arid land, they would stop at different towns along the way to rest, eat and refresh themselves. However, as they traveled, tensions grew between them. They began to argue and bicker over the smallest things, and soon their disagreements turned into a full-blown fight.

Their journey became even more difficult as they trudged through the sands of the desert, each man fuming with anger at the other. They were so consumed by their anger that they barely noticed the majestic scenery around them. They had both invested so much time and energy into their craft and they both felt that they were the better mason. They each believed that their skills and expertise were superior to the other, and this created a wedge between them.

The journey was long and grueling, and they were forced to

work together, even when they didn't want to. They traveled on horseback for many miles, stopping only when they needed to rest, eat and drink. However, they rarely spoke to each other, and when they did, it was only to argue and fight.

Finally, after a long and arduous journey, they arrived at the city. As they gazed upon the towering temple, they realized that their fight had been foolish and petty. They both felt ashamed for letting their anger get the better of them and for ruining their long-standing friendship. Hiram and Solomon looked at each other, and without a word, they embraced. They knew that their friendship was more important than any disagreement, and they pledged to never let anything come between them again.

Together, they began to work on the temple, using their mastery of masonry to create something truly remarkable. The work was grueling and backbreaking, but they persevered, knowing that the bond between them was unbreakable. As they worked side by side, they spoke about their journey and how they had let their petty argument get the best of them. They both agreed that it was foolish to fight over something so insignificant and that their friendship was more important than any disagreement. They realized that they had allowed their pride to get in the way, and it had almost cost them their friendship.

In the end, they completed the temple, and it stood as a testament to their friendship and the power of forgiveness. People from all over the land marveled at its grandeur and beauty, and Hiram and Solomon became known not just for their skill as masons, but also for their unwavering friendship.

They were hailed as the greatest master masons of their time, and people would often seek their services to build grand and beautiful structures. However, their friendship was the most valuable thing that they had, and they made sure to never let anything come between them again.

From that day on, they worked together on many other projects, always remembering the lesson they learned during their journey: that friendship is a treasure more valuable than any stone or building. They had learned that pride and anger can be destructive, and that forgiveness and humility are the keys to maintaining strong and lasting relationships. They knew that their journey had been an important and valuable lesson.

The Stonemason's Son: A Tale of Honor and Virtue

Long ago, in a small village nestled in the hills of a distant land, there lived a young boy named Ali. Ali's father was a renowned stonemason, and he had taken Ali on as his apprentice. Every day, Ali would follow his father to the quarry, where they would select the finest stones and carve them into beautiful works of art.

Ali loved his work, and he admired his father's skill and dedication to his craft. He was a bright and curious child, always eager to learn new techniques and improve his skills. His father was proud of his son's passion, and he taught him everything he knew about stonemasonry, from the basics of carving to the intricacies of design.

But despite his love for his work, Ali struggled with his relationship with his father. He felt that his father was too harsh and demanding, and he often found himself resenting his father's constant criticism and tough love. He longed for a kind word or a gesture of affection from his father, but he never received it.

One day, while working at the quarry, Ali stumbled upon a beautiful stone that he knew would make an exquisite sculpture. He took it to his father, hoping to impress him with his talent and creativity. But his father's response was unexpected.

"This is a fine stone," his father said, examining it closely. "But it is not enough. You must do better, Ali. You must always do better."

Ali was crushed by his father's words. He had hoped for praise and recognition, but all he had received was criticism and disappointment. He left the quarry, his heart heavy, and wandered aimlessly through the village.

As he walked, he came across an old woman struggling to carry a heavy load of firewood. She was stooped and frail, and Ali could see the pain etched on her face as she tried to lift the heavy load. Without a word, Ali rushed to her side and took the load from her, carrying it all the way to her doorstep.

The old woman was grateful, and she thanked Ali for his kindness. She asked him why he had helped her, and Ali replied simply, "It is the right thing to do. My father taught me to always do the right thing."

The old woman smiled, and her eyes twinkled with admiration. "Your father is a wise man," she said. "And you, my dear boy, are a kind and virtuous young man. Never forget the values he has taught you, and you will go far in this world."

Ali was taken aback by the old woman's words. He had never thought of himself as virtuous or kind, and he had certainly never heard anyone speak so highly of him. Her words gave him hope and courage, and he resolved to live up to the values his father had instilled in him.

From that day forward, Ali worked hard and tirelessly, carving the most beautiful sculptures his father had ever seen. And he always remembered the old woman's words, striving to be a kind and virtuous person, both in his work and in his relationships with others.

Over time, Ali's relationship with his father improved. He began to see that his father's criticism and tough love were not meant to hurt him, but to make him a better stonemason and a better person. And he knew that his father was proud of him, even if he never said it in so many words.

In the end, Ali became a great stonemason, known throughout the land for his skill, his dedication, and his kindness. And he knew that he owed it all to his father, who had taught him the importance of hard work, perseverance, and the values of honor and virtue. As Ali grew older and took on apprentices of his own, he passed down his father's teachings and values to the next generation of stonemasons. He knew that his success was not just his own, but the product of the lessons he had learned from his father and the community around him.

Years passed, and Ali's father grew old and frail. One day, while Ali was working in his shop, his father appeared at the door, looking weak and tired. Ali rushed to his father's side, helping him to a seat and offering him water and food. As they sat together, Ali's father looked up at him with pride and love in his eyes.

"My son," he said, "you have become a great man, a skilled stonemason, and a true example of honor and virtue. I am proud of all that you have accomplished, and I know that you will continue to make me proud for generations to come."

Tears welled up in Ali's eyes as he embraced his father. He

knew that he had finally earned his father's respect and love, and he felt a deep sense of gratitude for all that his father had done for him.

In the years that followed, Ali continued to live his life by the values his father had taught him. He became a leader in his community, helping those in need and inspiring others to follow in his footsteps. And when he passed away, his legacy lived on, not just in the beautiful sculptures he had created, but in the countless lives he had touched and inspired through his kindness, his honor, and his unwavering commitment to virtue.

The Craftsman's Prodigy: Micah's Pursuit of Perfection

In the bustling city of Bethel, there lived a young boy named Micah. Micah's father was a carpenter who worked tirelessly to provide for his family. From a young age, Micah was fascinated by his father's work and spent every moment he could watching him create intricate wooden carvings and furniture.

One day, while Micah was wandering through the marketplace, he came across a group of craftsmen working on a grand project. The project was a magnificent temple that was being built to honor the Lord. Micah was in awe of the masterful work that the craftsmen were doing. He watched as they carefully measured and cut each piece of stone, fitting them together with precision.

Micah was so captivated by the work that he decided to approach the master craftsman and ask if he could become his apprentice. The master craftsman, impressed by Micah's passion and dedication, agreed to take him on as his apprentice.

Micah worked tirelessly alongside the master craftsman, learning everything he could about stonework and the art of building. He was a quick learner, and soon he was creating intricate carvings and designs that even the master craftsman was impressed with.

Despite his young age, Micah had a natural talent for stonework, and he was constantly striving for perfection in his craft. He would spend hours practicing and honing his skills, determined to create something truly remarkable.

As the temple neared completion, Micah was given the task of creating the most important piece of the temple - the altar. It was a challenging task, but Micah was determined to create something that would be worthy of the Lord.

For weeks, Micah worked tirelessly on the altar, meticulously carving every detail with precision and care. He poured his heart and soul into the project, and finally, the day came when the altar was unveiled to the public.

The people of Bethel were in awe of Micah's creation. The altar was a masterpiece, with intricate carvings and designs that were unlike anything they had ever seen before. Even the master craftsman was impressed with Micah's work, declaring that he was truly a prodigy.

From that day on, Micah's reputation as a skilled craftsman spread throughout the land. People from far and wide came to seek out his work, and he became known as one of the greatest craftsmen in all the land.

But despite his success, Micah never lost his passion for stonework. He continued to work tirelessly, always striving for perfection in everything he created. And in the end, it was his unwavering dedication and commitment to his craft that truly made him a prodigy.

The Redemption of Saban: A Mason's Tale of Regret and Forgiveness

Saban had always been a skilled apprentice mason, learning the trade from his father and his grandfather before him. But as he grew older, he became increasingly focused on making a name for himself, and he began to take shortcuts in his work, cutting corners to finish jobs quickly and earn more money.

It wasn't long before Saban's work started to suffer, and his clients began to notice. Many complained about the shoddy workmanship and the lack of attention to detail. Saban tried to ignore their complaints, telling himself that he was still a skilled mason and that he could fix any mistakes that he had made.

But as the years went by, Saban's mistakes began to pile up, and he found himself overwhelmed by regret. He knew that he had taken the easy way out, that he had let his pride and his greed get the best of him, and that he had betrayed the trust of those who had hired him.

Saban tried to make amends, but it was too late. Many of his clients refused to work with him again, and his reputation as a mason was in ruins. He felt ashamed and alone, and he began to wonder if there was any way to redeem himself.

One day, Saban heard about a wise teacher who was travelling through the countryside, offering guidance to those who sought it. Saban decided to seek out this teacher, hoping that he might be able to find some answers.

When Saban found the teacher, he poured out his heart,

confessing his mistakes and his regrets, and asking for forgiveness. The teacher listened patiently, and then he spoke.

"My friend, you have already taken the first step on the path to redemption," he said. "You have recognized your mistakes, and you have come seeking guidance. But there is more that you must do."

The teacher then told Saban a parable about a man who had squandered his wealth and his talents, but who had been given a second chance to redeem himself. The man had worked tirelessly to make amends for his past mistakes, and in the end, he had found forgiveness and a new sense of purpose.

Saban listened intently to the story, and he felt a glimmer of hope. He knew that he had a long journey ahead of him, but he also knew that he was not alone. With the teacher's guidance, he began to work diligently to make amends for his past mistakes, striving to become the skilled and honest mason that he had once been.

It wasn't easy, and there were many times when Saban felt discouraged. But he persevered, and he gradually began to rebuild his reputation and his sense of self-worth. And as he worked, he felt a sense of peace and joy that he had never known before.

In the end, Saban knew that he would never be able to undo the mistakes of his past. But he also knew that he had been given a second chance to live with honesty and integrity, and to use his skills for the greater good. And for that, he was truly grateful.

The Redemption of Hiira

In the land of Israel, during the time of King Solomon, there was a skilled and experienced master mason named Hiira. He had been one of the lead architects tasked with constructing the grand and magnificent Temple of Solomon, which was to be a place of worship and reverence for the people of Israel.

However, Hiira had a serious flaw that hindered his work - he had a bad attitude. He was constantly complaining, criticizing, and causing tension with his fellow craftsmen. He believed that his skills were superior to everyone else's and that he did not need anyone else's help to complete the task.

As a result of his poor behavior, King Solomon was forced to demote Hiira from his position as a lead foreman, and he was removed from working on the Temple. Hiira was devastated and ashamed of his actions, and he felt that he had lost his sense of purpose in life.

For many months, Hiira wandered the streets of Jerusalem, feeling lost and alone. But one day, he came across a group of poor and destitute people who were in desperate need of shelter. Hiira felt compelled to help them, and he used his masonry skills to build small homes and shelters for them.

As he worked on these humble structures, Hiira realized the true meaning of his craft. He understood that his talents were not just for personal glory or recognition but were meant to serve others and help them in their time of need. He also learned the importance of having a good attitude, working cooperatively with others, and treating everyone with respect and kindness.

With this newfound realization, Hiira went back to King Solomon and humbly apologized for his past behavior. He asked for a second chance to work on the Temple, promising to be a positive and productive member of the team.

King Solomon, impressed by Hiira's change of heart, welcomed him back to the project. Hiira worked tirelessly with his fellow craftsmen, putting his newfound humility and positive attitude to work. Together, they completed the Temple, and it was even more magnificent than anyone had imagined.

Hiram's journey teaches us all an important lesson in humility, and how the power of redemption and forgiveness can transform us into better people.

The Envious Lament of Ailel

In the Xaster village, there lived a man named Ailel who was known for his hard work and honesty. However, he was also known for his envy and jealousy towards his neighbors who were living prosperous lives. Ailel often looked around and wondered why God had made him suffer so much while others around him were blessed with wealth and success.

Ailel's envy grew more and more each day, and he began to despise his neighbors for their good fortune. He started to speak ill of them behind their backs, and his bitterness and resentment towards them began to affect his relationships with others in the village. Despite his efforts, his situation never improved, and he remained poor and struggling.

One day, a wealthy merchant came to the village, looking for someone to work for him. The merchant noticed Ailel's hard work and honesty and offered him a job. Ailel saw this as a chance to finally make something of himself and accepted the offer.

Over time, Ailel became successful in his work and started earning a lot of money. He built himself a big house, bought vast lands and accumulated great wealth. Ailel was no longer poor, and he no longer envied his neighbors. However, his past actions had already left a mark on the community.

His neighbors, who had once been his friends, no longer trusted him or welcomed him into their homes. They remembered how he had spoken ill of them and how he had been jealous of their good fortune. Ailel had isolated himself from the community, and he realized that his envy and jealousy had caused him to lose sight of what was truly important in life.

One day, during a community gathering, Ailel publicly apologized to his neighbors for his past behavior and asked for their forgiveness. He told them that his envy and jealousy had blinded him, and he was ashamed of his actions. To his surprise, his neighbors forgave him and welcomed him back into the community.

Ailel was happy to be back in the good graces of his neighbors, but he soon discovered that his wealth and prosperity had also attracted the attention of bandits who roamed the countryside. One night, while Ailel was sleeping, the bandits raided his house and stole all of his possessions, leaving him with nothing but the clothes on his back.

Ailel was devastated and cried out to God, asking why he had lost everything he had worked so hard for. He realized that his envy and jealousy had caused him to lose sight of what was truly important in life, and he had to pay the price for his actions.

Despite his loss, Ailel found peace in his humility and his renewed faith in God. He lived the rest of his life as a humble servant of God, never again giving in to envy or jealousy. He worked hard and earned an honest living, and he was content with what he had. And thus, Ailel's story became a cautionary tale of the dangers of envy and the importance of humility in the eyes of God.

Years later, when Ailel passed away, the villagers remembered him not for his wealth or success but for his humility and his kindness towards others. His story was passed down from generation to generation as a reminder of the consequences of envy and the importance of living a humble and honest life.

Viali's Folly: The Danger of Presumption

Once upon a time in the village of Xaster, there was a farmer named Viali. He was a hardworking man who had spent his entire life cultivating his fields. Viali was known to be an optimistic person, always looking for the bright side of things. This year, he had reason to be more optimistic than usual. The summer had been long and hot, and the rains had come at the right time. The crops were growing tall and strong, and it looked like it was going to be a bountiful harvest.

Viali had always dreamed of having a huge crop, and it looked like his dream was finally coming true. He started planning what he was going to do with all the extra money he was going to make. He would finally be able to build that bigger house he had always wanted, and he would have enough left over to buy more land and hire more workers.

As the summer turned to fall, Viali's excitement grew. He could hardly wait for the harvest. One day, as he was walking through his fields, he noticed a few ears of corn that looked a little different from the others. They were fully ripe and ready to be picked, so he decided to harvest them early.

To his dismay, Viali found that the corn was not fully developed. It was tough and inedible. He realized that he had made a mistake in assuming that the rest of the crop was going to be as good as those few ears of corn. He had let his excitement get the best of him, and he had counted his chickens before they hatched.

As the weeks went on, Viali's excitement turned to despair. The rest of the crop was not as good as he had hoped. The corn was stunted, the wheat was full of chaff, and the vegetables were small and underdeveloped. He had made the mistake of assuming that everything was going to be perfect, and he had not taken into account the many variables that could affect the harvest.

Viali had to face the fact that his greed and presumption had cost him dearly. He had let his dreams of wealth and prosperity cloud his judgment, and he had failed to appreciate the hard work and dedication that it took to grow a good crop. He learned that he could not take anything for granted, and that he needed to work hard and be vigilant in order to succeed.

In the end, Viali's folly became a lesson for the entire village. People learned that they should never count their chickens before they hatch, and that they should always be humble and grateful for what they had. And Viali, having learned his lesson, redoubled his efforts and went on to become one of the most respected farmers in the village of Xaster.

Xial Village

In the small village of Xial, located in the hills of Judea, the people were known for their strong work ethic. They spent most of their days tending to their fields and animals, and they worked tirelessly from sunrise to sunset, every day of the week. They believed that hard work was necessary to provide for their families and to ensure that their crops and animals thrived.

One day, a traveler passed through Xial and noticed how serious and busy the villagers were. He asked them why they worked so hard all the time, and they replied, "We have no other choice. If we don't work hard, we won't be able to provide for our families, and our crops and animals won't thrive."

The traveler nodded his head and continued on his journey. However, as he traveled, he came across another village where the people were singing, dancing, and playing games. They seemed carefree and happy, and the traveler was surprised to see that they had just as much food and resources as the people of Xial.

Intrigued, the traveler returned to Xial and shared his observations with the villagers. "I saw another village where the people were happy and carefree, even though they work just as hard as you do," he said. "Perhaps there is a time for work and a time for play."

The people of Xial were skeptical at first. They had never heard of such a thing as taking a break from work. But eventually, they decided to take the traveler's advice and set aside a day each week for rest and relaxation. On this day, they put down their tools, closed their shops, and spent time with their families and friends. They sang, danced, played games, and enjoyed good food and conversation.

At first, the villagers felt guilty for taking a break from their work. They worried that they were being lazy or neglecting their responsibilities. But as they began to embrace this day of rest, they realized that it was just as important as their work. It gave them time to rejuvenate, to connect with loved ones, and to appreciate the beauty of the world around them.

Over time, the people of Xial found that their work was even more productive and fulfilling because they had learned the value of rest and play. They had discovered that there was a time for work and a time for play, and both were necessary for a happy and healthy life.

The village of Xial began to thrive in new ways. The people were happier and more connected to one another, and their crops and animals seemed to thrive even more than before. They had learned an important lesson about the balance between work and play.

From that day forward, the people of Xial continued to work hard, but they also made time for rest and relaxation. They knew that life was not just about working hard, but about enjoying the simple pleasures of life and spending time with the people they loved. And as a result, their lives were richer, more fulfilling, and more joyful.

The Deceitful Brother: A Lesson on the Consequences of Cheating

Once there was a man named Jacob who was known for being cunning and deceitful. He had a twin brother named Esau, and Jacob was always jealous of him. One day, Esau was very hungry and came to Jacob, begging for some of the stew he was cooking. Jacob saw an opportunity to take advantage of his brother's hunger and offered to give him some stew in exchange for his birthright - the inheritance that would make him the head of their family.

Esau, not thinking clearly because of his hunger, agreed to the deal and gave up his birthright. Jacob had cheated his own brother and taken something that was not rightfully his. But Jacob's deceit did not stop there. Later on, when their father Isaac was old and blind, he wanted to give his blessings to his eldest son, Esau. But Jacob, knowing that he was not the chosen son, pretended to be Esau by covering himself in animal skins and tricked his father into giving him the blessings meant for his brother.

Esau was furious when he found out what had happened and vowed to kill Jacob. Jacob had to flee from his home and live in fear for many years, always looking over his shoulder and never feeling truly safe.

In the end, Jacob learned a valuable lesson. He realized that cheating would not bring him true happiness or success. Instead, it only brought him trouble and caused him to lose the trust of those around him. Jacob had to work hard to earn back the trust and forgiveness of his family, and it was a long and difficult process.

The story of Jacob and Esau teaches us that cheating will not get you anything in the end. If you cheat, you will eventually pay the price for your actions, whether it's through the loss of relationships, reputation, or something else. Honesty and hard work may take longer, but they will bring you true success and happiness in the long run.

The Quarryman's Reflection

Once upon a time, in the ancient land of Israel, there was a man named Simon. Simon was a hardworking quarryman who spent most of his days chiseling away at the stones to provide for his family. He was known throughout the land for his strength and his determination to get the job done.

One day, Simon was tasked with creating a large stone for the temple. He worked tirelessly, day and night, to craft the perfect stone. After several days of work, Simon finally finished the stone and presented it to the overseer. The overseer inspected the stone and, to Simon's horror, found a small crack running through the middle.

Simon was devastated. He had worked so hard and put so much effort into the stone. He couldn't believe that he had made such a simple mistake. He knew that he would have to start all over again.

As Simon trudged back to his home, he couldn't help but think about what had gone wrong. He had acted too quickly and hadn't taken the time to think through his actions. He knew that he needed to learn from his mistake and make sure that he didn't make the same mistake twice.

Over the next few days, Simon spent his time reflecting on his mistake. He realized that he needed to take the time to think through his actions before acting. He knew that by doing so, he would be able to avoid making simple mistakes like the one he had made.

With his new understanding of the value of thoughtful action, Simon returned to the quarry. He worked diligently, taking his time to think through each action before taking it. He double-checked his work and made sure that he was doing everything correctly.

Several days later, Simon presented the overseer with another stone. This time, the overseer inspected it and found it to be flawless. Simon had taken the time to think through his actions, and it had paid off.

From that day forward, Simon became known not just for his strength but also for his wisdom. He had learned a valuable lesson about the importance of never acting before you think, and he had become a better man for it.

The Lesson of Othan: The Importance of Observing, Listening, and Learning

In the ancient city of Jerusalem, there lived a young apprentice mason named Othan. He was known for his skill in carving and shaping stones, but he had a flaw that often got him into trouble. Othan was very talkative and tended to speak before he listened. He always had an opinion and was quick to offer advice, even when it was not needed.

One day, Othan was tasked with working on a grand temple, alongside some of the most experienced masons in the city. Othan was thrilled to work on such a prestigious project and was eager to show off his skills. However, he quickly found himself struggling to keep up with the pace of his more experienced colleagues. He would often make mistakes and had to redo his work multiple times, which led to delays in the project.

One afternoon, Othan was working on a particularly tricky stone carving, and his chisel slipped, causing a chip on the surface of the stone. Frustrated and embarrassed, Othan began to curse and complain loudly. One of the older masons, who had been observing Othan's work, walked over and asked him what had happened.

Othan quickly explained his mistake and how he was struggling with the carving. The older mason nodded and then said, "You know, Othan, sometimes it's better to be quiet and listen. Watch how we work and observe our techniques. You can learn a lot by simply paying attention and taking the time to listen and learn."

At first, Othan was taken aback by the mason's words. He had never considered that his constant talking and lack of observation could be the cause of his struggles. However, he took the advice to heart and began to focus more on observing the other masons, watching how they worked and learning from their techniques.

Over time, Othan's work improved, and he became much more efficient in his carving and shaping. He began to listen more and speak less, and as a result, he learned valuable lessons that helped him to grow and develop his skills. He also gained a newfound respect from his colleagues, who saw how he had transformed into a more skilled and mature craftsman.

In the end, Othan learned a valuable lesson about the importance of observing, listening, and learning. He realized that sometimes the best way to become wise is to be quiet and pay attention to the wisdom of others. From that day forward, Othan became known as one of the most skilled and respected masons in the city, all because he learned to be more observant and to listen more than he spoke.

The Tale of Elijah and the Humble Beggar

Elijah was a man who was loved by all in his small village. He was known for his wisdom, compassion, and kindness towards everyone he met. He would often walk through the village, stopping to chat with anyone who caught his eye. He believed that everyone had a story worth hearing and would often spend hours listening to the tales of the villagers.

One day, as he was walking through the village, he saw a beggar sitting by the side of the road. The beggar was old and ragged, and his clothes were torn and dirty. He looked up at Elijah with tired eyes and held out a cup, hoping for some spare change.

Elijah paused for a moment, studying the beggar's face. He could sense a kind heart behind the wrinkles and grime, and he felt compelled to help him. Instead of giving the beggar some coins, Elijah took a seat beside him and struck up a conversation.

"Tell me, friend," he said, "what is it that you truly desire in life?"

The beggar looked at him with surprise. "Why do you ask such a question?" he said. "Surely you can see that all I need is a few coins to survive."

Elijah smiled. "I see more than that," he said. "I see a man who has lived a long and difficult life, who has faced hardships and struggles that most of us could not imagine. But I also see a man who has a wealth of experience and knowledge, and who could teach us all a great deal if we were willing to listen."

The beggar looked down, ashamed. He had never thought of himself as anything more than a beggar, and he had never imagined that anyone would see him as anything else. But as he listened to Elijah's words, he began to see himself in a different light.

"I have lived a hard life," he said, "but I have also learned many things along the way. I have seen the beauty of the world, even in its darkest moments. And I have come to understand that there is more to life than money and possessions."

Elijah nodded. "You speak the truth," he said. "And I believe that there are many who could benefit from your wisdom. Will you come with me to the village square and share your story with those who pass by?"

The beggar hesitated, unsure if he was ready to face the judgment of others. But something in Elijah's eyes gave him courage, and he nodded his agreement.

Together, the two men walked to the village square, where a crowd of people had already gathered. Elijah stepped forward and introduced the beggar, telling them of his own encounter with the wise man.

The beggar took a deep breath and began to speak. He told them of his struggles and his triumphs, of the lessons he had learned along the way. He spoke of the kindness of strangers, the beauty of the natural world, and the importance of gratitude and compassion.

As he spoke, the people listened with rapt attention, hanging on his every word. They had never expected to hear such wisdom from a simple beggar, but they could see now that Elijah had been right all along. There was more to this man than met the eye, and they were grateful for the lessons he had shared.

When the beggar finished speaking, the crowd erupted into applause. They had been touched by his words and were eager to hear more. The beggar continued to share his wisdom with the villagers, and they began to see him in a new light. He was no longer seen as a burden on society, but as a wise teacher whose words were worth more than gold.

The Tale of Anom

Long ago, in the land of Israel, there was a small village called Anom. It was a peaceful village nestled in a valley surrounded by lush green hills. The villagers of Anom were hardworking and content with their simple way of life. They cultivated crops, tended to their livestock, and engaged in handicrafts to earn a living. Despite their modest lifestyle, the villagers were happy and content with their lot.

However, there was one thing they always wished for but could never have - a steady supply of fresh water. The village was situated far away from any natural water source, and the villagers had to travel long distances to fetch water from a nearby river. The journey was not only tiresome but also dangerous, as they had to cross dense forests and rocky terrain. Despite their hardships, the villagers remained grateful for the little water they could get and never complained.

One day, a wealthy merchant named Armand came to Anom with a proposal. He offered to build a canal that would bring water from a nearby spring to the village. The villagers were overjoyed at the thought of having a reliable source of water and eagerly agreed to the merchant's proposal.

Armand began the construction of the canal, and the villagers watched with excitement as the project progressed. The work was grueling, and Armand had to employ many workers to excavate the canal through the rugged terrain. However, the villagers soon realized that the construction was taking much longer than they had anticipated, and the cost of the project was increasing. The workers toiled under the hot sun and the villagers grew impatient with the slow progress. They began to take the project for granted and stopped appreciating the effort put in by the merchant. The villagers grumbled and complained, demanding that the canal be completed quickly.

Armand, on the other hand, was determined to complete the project, despite the challenges. He knew that the canal was essential for the survival of the village, and he worked tirelessly to ensure its completion. He invested his own money and resources into the project, even when it seemed like it would never be finished.

Months turned into years, and the canal remained unfinished. The villagers grew restless and frustrated, and many of them began to lose hope that the canal would ever be completed. They started to complain about the delay, and some even questioned the merchant's intentions.

However, Armand never gave up. He continued to work on the canal day and night, even when the workers grew tired and wanted to quit. He was determined to see the project through to the end, no matter what.

Finally, after years of hard work and dedication, the canal was completed. The villagers rejoiced as water flowed into their village, and they no longer had to struggle to fetch water. They marveled at the ingenuity and skill that had gone into constructing the canal, and they realized how fortunate they were to have a source of water that was reliable and abundant.

The merchant was pleased with his accomplishment and happy to see the villagers' joy. He had not only provided them with a valuable resource but also taught them a valuable lesson. The villagers of Anom learned that nothing worth having comes easy and that sometimes we must be patient and persevere through hardships to achieve our goals. They learned the importance of gratitude and appreciation, and they promised to always remember the hard work and dedication that went into building the canal.

From that day on, the village of Anom prospered. The villagers were able to grow more crops, and they had more time to engage in other activities. The canal had transformed their lives and had made their village a better place to live. The Tale of Anom became a legend in Xaster, reminding people to be grateful for what they have and never to take anything for granted. The canal had taught the villagers of Anom a valuable lesson, one that they would never forget.

The Downfall of Greed: A Lesson from David's Apprenticeship

David was a young apprentice mason who lived in the ancient city of Jerusalem during the reign of King Solomon. David had always been fascinated by the art of masonry and dreamed of one day building a great structure that would stand the test of time.

One day, David was given the opportunity to work on the construction of the magnificent Temple of Jerusalem. He was thrilled to be a part of such an important project and worked tirelessly to ensure that every stone was placed with care and precision.

As the construction of the temple progressed, David noticed that some of the other workers were becoming increasingly greedy. They began stealing precious stones and hoarding them for themselves, even though they had already been paid for their work.

David knew that this was wrong and tried to speak out against their actions, but he was met with resistance and even hostility from his fellow workers. They told him that he was foolish to pass up such an opportunity to enrich himself.

However, David remained steadfast in his principles and refused to take part in their greed. He continued to work hard and was eventually recognized for his skill and dedication by King Solomon himself.

In the end, the greedy workers were caught and punished for their misdeeds, while David's honesty and integrity were rewarded. He was given the opportunity to lead his own team of masons and was even entrusted with overseeing the construction of the temple's most important and ornate features.

David realized that his commitment to doing what was right had not only earned him the respect of his peers, but had also led to his own success and happiness. He learned that greed would always lead to downfall, and that the true measure of a person's worth was not in what they possessed, but in their actions and character.

The Unbreakable Mason: Aeral's Lesson in Unity

In the ancient land of Canaan, there was a master mason named Aeral. He was renowned throughout the region for his skill in building strong and durable structures that could withstand even the toughest of weather conditions. Aeral was proud of his work and had a reputation for being able to build anything, no matter how challenging the task.

One day, the people of Canaan decided to build a great wall around their city to protect themselves from their enemies. They called upon Aeral to build the wall, knowing he was the best mason in the land. Aeral was excited about the project and quickly got to work.

As he began to build, Aeral soon realized that the task was much more challenging than he had anticipated. He encountered numerous obstacles, and his progress was slow. Aeral became frustrated and started to doubt his abilities. He had always thought that his strength as a mason came from his individual skill and ability. However, as he struggled with the wall, he realized that he needed help.

One day, as he was working, a group of travelers passed by. They saw Aeral's struggle and offered to help him. Aeral was hesitant at first, but he eventually accepted their offer, realizing that he could not do it alone. The travelers worked alongside Aeral, each bringing their unique skills to the task. Some were strong and able to lift heavy stones, while others were skilled in carving intricate designs.

Together, they built the wall, and it was the strongest and most beautiful structure that Aeral had ever built. As they worked, Aeral began to understand the value of working together as a team. He realized that each person had something to contribute, and together, they could accomplish much more than any one person could alone.

As they finished the wall, Aeral looked at the travelers who had helped him and thanked them for their assistance. He offered to pay them for their services, but they refused, saying that they had worked together for the common good, and that was payment enough.

Aeral learned an important lesson from the travelers. He realized that his individual skill and ability were only part of the equation. He had always prided himself on being a master mason, but now he saw himself as part of a larger community of builders. He understood that there was strength in unity, and that when people worked together, they could accomplish great things.

From that day on, Aeral worked differently. He no longer saw himself as the master mason, but as part of a larger community of builders. He always remembered the lesson he had learned, that there was strength in unity, and that together, people could achieve great things.

The people of Canaan were amazed at the strength and beauty of the wall that Aeral and the travelers had built. They saw the value of working together as a community and began to apply this lesson to other aspects of their lives. They realized that when they worked together, they could accomplish anything, no matter how challenging the task. The wall that Aeral and the travelers had built became a symbol of the power of unity and served as a reminder to the people of Canaan that they were stronger together than they were alone.

The Stone of Brotherhood: Abel's Lesson in Kindness

In the land of Nod, Abel was a young apprentice mason who was passionate about his work. He dreamed of becoming a master craftsman and spent long hours chiseling and shaping stone with precision and care, always striving for perfection.

One day, Abel was working on a large building project when he accidentally dropped a heavy stone on his foot. He let out a cry of pain, and his fellow apprentices rushed to his aid. However, instead of offering sympathy and help, they began to laugh and mock him, calling him clumsy and foolish.

Abel felt embarrassed and hurt by their words. He was struggling with the pain in his foot and didn't need their ridicule on top of that. He retreated to a quiet corner of the worksite to nurse his injured foot, feeling ashamed and alone.

As he sat there, he noticed a small stone lying nearby. He absentmindedly picked it up and began to polish it with his shirt sleeve. He had always enjoyed working with stones and was fascinated by their unique shapes and colors. As he polished the stone, he thought about the way his fellow apprentices had treated him. He realized that he had often been guilty of the same kind of unkindness and mockery towards others. He felt ashamed of himself and resolved to change his ways and treat others with the same kindness and respect that he would like to be shown.

As he continued to polish the stone, he noticed that it had a unique shape and color. He saw the potential for it to become a beautiful piece of artwork. Inspired by his newfound commitment to kindness, he decided to carve the stone into a symbol of brotherhood and unity. He spent long hours carefully chiseling the stone, shaping it into a beautiful, intricate design. He wanted to create something that would remind him and others to always treat each other with love and respect.

Weeks passed, and Abel's foot healed, but the memory of his experience and his newfound commitment to kindness stayed with him. He completed his apprenticeship and eventually became a master mason, renowned for his skill and artistry. He always kept the Stone of Brotherhood close at hand, a symbol of the lesson he had learned and a reminder to treat others with kindness and respect.

Years passed, and Abel's reputation as a master craftsman grew. One day, a wealthy merchant approached him with a request to build a grand cathedral. Abel accepted the challenge, and the merchant provided him with all the materials he needed, including a large shipment of rare and expensive stones.

As Abel and his team began work on the cathedral, he noticed that the other workers were not treating the expensive stones with the same care and respect that he had been taught. They were rough and careless with the stones, handling them with little regard for their value. Abel realized that he had an opportunity to teach them the lesson he had learned all those years ago.

He called a meeting with the workers and showed them the Stone of Brotherhood, explaining its significance and the lesson it had taught him. He urged them to treat all the stones they worked with, including the rare and expensive ones, with the same care and respect they would like to be shown. He challenged them to work together, to treat each other with kindness and respect, and to create something truly beautiful.

The workers were inspired by Abel's words and embraced his challenge. They began to work together with greater care and attention to detail. They treated each other with kindness and respect, and the atmosphere on the worksite changed for the better. The cathedral they built was a masterpiece of beauty and craftsmanship, a testament to the lesson of kindness and brotherhood that Abel had learned so many years ago.

The Truth Carved in Stone: Samuel's Journey of Honesty

In a small village nestled in the hills of ancient Israel, a young man named Samuel had just begun his apprenticeship as a mason. He had always been fascinated by the art of stone carving and was eager to learn from his master, Eli.

One day, while working on a particularly challenging piece of stone, Samuel accidentally chipped off a small piece from the corner of the block. Fearing the wrath of his master, he tried to cover up the mistake by smoothing over the area with his chisel.

But as Samuel worked on the stone, he realized that the blemish could still be seen, no matter how hard he tried to hide it. Suddenly, he heard a voice in his head, urging him to tell the truth and confess his mistake.

Samuel knew that he had to make things right, no matter the consequences. He went to Eli and confessed his error, fully expecting to be scolded or even punished for his carelessness.

To Samuel's surprise, Eli was impressed by his honesty and integrity. Instead of punishing him, he praised Samuel for his bravery and rewarded him with a new block of stone to work on, this time with even greater care and precision.

As Samuel worked on his new project, he felt a sense of pride and accomplishment that he had never experienced before. He realized that the truth was like the stone he was carving - it was unyielding and unchanging, but also beautiful and powerful when used with care and skill.

Years later, Samuel became a master mason himself and passed on his wisdom to his own apprentices. He taught them that honesty was the foundation of all great work, and that the truth could be carved into stone for all time, a legacy that would endure for generations to come.

The Stone that Stumbled: Jesiah's Lesson in Humility

In the land of Judah, there lived a young and ambitious apprentice mason named Jesiah. He had always been skilled with his hands, and had dreamed of building a great tower that would reach the heavens. He believed that with his skill and determination, he alone could make this vision a reality.

Jesiah worked tirelessly, day and night, chiseling away at the stones and laying them in place. As the tower grew taller, he became more and more proud of his work. He boasted to his fellow craftsmen about his skill and his vision for the tower, and believed that he alone could bring it to completion.

But in his pride, Jesiah became careless. He began to take shortcuts, rushing through the more difficult sections of the tower without considering the consequences of his actions. He ignored the advice and feedback of his fellow craftsmen, believing that he knew best.

One day, as he was working on a particularly tricky section of the tower, Jesiah stumbled and dropped a heavy stone. It rolled down the tower and crashed to the ground, narrowly missing a group of workers below.

Shaken by the incident, Jesiah realized that his pride and arrogance had caused him to overlook the importance of humility and caution. He knew that if he continued down this path, he would put the safety of the tower and its workers in jeopardy.

Desperate for guidance, Jesiah sought counsel from an elder

mason, who had seen many young craftsmen fall prey to the same arrogance and overconfidence that had befallen Jesiah. The elder listened to Jesiah's story and advised him to reflect on the story of the Tower of Babel, where the people had become so prideful that they believed they could build a tower to the heavens, only to be humbled by God.

Jesiah took the elder's words to heart and began to work with greater care and humility. He learned to listen to the advice and feedback of his fellow craftsmen, and to put the needs of the tower and the safety of its workers above his own ambitions.

Over time, Jesiah's attitude changed, and he began to see the value in collaboration and communication. He no longer believed that he alone held the key to the tower's success, but instead recognized the importance of working together as a team.

As the tower neared completion, Jesiah looked back on his journey and realized that it was his stumble that had led him to this newfound wisdom and humility. He was grateful for the lesson he had learned and knew that he would carry it with him for the rest of his days.

And so, the Tower of Judah stood tall, a testament not only to the skill and craftsmanship of its builders, but also to the importance of humility and caution in all of our endeavors. Jesiah had learned the hard way that even the most skilled and talented among us can stumble, but it is through humility and a willingness to learn that we can rise again, stronger and wiser than before.

The Tale of Hilath: Lessons in Honesty and the Perils of Deceit

In the village of Xaster, there lived a young boy named Hilath. Hilath was known for his intelligence, quick wit, and playful nature, but he was also notorious for his love of pranks and trickery. He would often play practical jokes on his friends and family, leaving them confused and frustrated.

One day, Hilath's pranks went too far. He decided to play a trick on the village elder, telling him a false story about a wild boar that had been terrorizing the village. The elder, concerned for the safety of his people, immediately ordered a hunting party to go after the boar.

As it turned out, there was no wild boar. Hilath had made up the story just to see if he could fool the elder. When the hunting party returned empty-handed, the elder was furious. He summoned Hilath and demanded an explanation.

At first, Hilath tried to deny any wrongdoing. But as the elder pressed him for the truth, Hilath realized the gravity of his actions. He confessed to making up the story about the wild boar, and he begged for forgiveness.

The elder, however, was not so forgiving. He saw Hilath's prank as a serious breach of trust, and he decided to punish him severely. Hilath was banished from the village and forced to live alone in the wilderness for a year.

During his time in the wilderness, Hilath had plenty of time to reflect on his actions. He realized that his love of pranks had blinded him to the consequences of his actions. He understood the importance of honesty and the perils of deceit.

Hilath spent his days hunting and gathering food, building shelter, and reflecting on his mistakes. He often thought about the people he had hurt and how he could make things right. He knew that he had to do something to regain the trust of his community.

As the year of exile drew to a close, Hilath decided to make amends. He set out to find the wild boar that he had made up in his prank. He hoped that by proving himself capable of tracking and hunting a real boar, he could redeem himself in the eyes of the village elder and the community.

It was a difficult and dangerous journey, but Hilath was determined to succeed. He faced many challenges along the way, including harsh weather, dangerous animals, and difficult terrain. But he persevered, and after many weeks of searching, he finally found the wild boar.

Hilath hunted the boar with skill and precision. He tracked it through the forest, set traps, and finally brought it down with a single arrow. It was a difficult and dangerous task, but Hilath felt a sense of satisfaction and pride in his accomplishment.

With the boar's carcass slung over his shoulder, Hilath returned to the village. He presented the boar to the village elder and the hunting party as proof of his skill and determination. He apologized for his prank and asked for forgiveness.

At first, the elder and the hunting party were skeptical. They saw Hilath's actions as a desperate attempt to regain their trust. But as Hilath spoke from the heart, they began to see a genuine remorse and a newfound sense of responsibility.

The village elder forgave Hilath, and the hunting party welcomed him back into the community. But Hilath knew that forgiveness was not enough. He knew that he had to earn back the trust of his friends and family.

Hilath spent the next several years working tirelessly to make amends. He volunteered for community service, helped his neighbors with their chores, and offered his skills and knowledge to anyone who needed it. He became known as a trustworthy and dependable member of the community.

The tale of Hilath teaches us the importance of honesty and the consequences of deceit. Hilath's journey from prankster to responsible member of the community was a long and difficult one, but it ultimately led him to a greater understanding of the value of trust and the importance of accountability.

Through his experiences, Hilath learned that a single lie or prank can have far-reaching consequences that can damage relationships and erode trust. He also learned that it takes time and effort to earn back the trust of others once it has been broken.

The story of Hilath serves as a cautionary tale to all of us. We must be mindful of our words and actions and strive to be honest and forthright in all our dealings with others. We must also be willing to accept responsibility for our mistakes and work to make things right when we have caused harm.

At the same time, the story of Hilath also offers hope and inspiration. It shows us that even when we make mistakes, we have the ability to learn from them, grow as individuals, and ultimately become better people.

In the end, Hilath's journey teaches us that honesty and integrity are essential qualities for a happy and successful life. It reminds us that our actions have consequences, and that we must be mindful of the impact we have on others. And it encourages us to strive for personal growth, even in the face of adversity and setbacks.

Jerah's Fear: A Tale of Success and Regret in the Village of Caleth

In the ancient village of Caleth, nestled among the rolling hills of Israel, there lived a man named Jerah. He was known throughout the village and the surrounding region as a successful businessman and farmer, having built up his wealth and reputation through years of hard work and dedication.

Jerah was a man who was deeply driven by his fear of failure. He believed that his success was the only thing that gave him worth and that if he failed, he would be nothing. This fear consumed him, and he never allowed himself to rest or relax, always pushing himself to work harder and achieve more.

Jerah was always the first one to arrive at the fields in the morning and the last to leave at night. He was constantly thinking about his business, strategizing ways to improve his crop yields, and expand his operations. His mind was always racing with thoughts of what he needed to do next, and he rarely took a moment to appreciate the beauty of the world around him.

Despite his reputation for success, many of the villagers pitied Jerah, sensing that his life was devoid of true happiness and contentment. They saw the lines etched deep into his face, the furrowed brow, and the constant tension in his muscles. They knew that Jerah's fear was what drove him, and they worried that it would ultimately be his downfall.

One day, a wise old man came to the village, and Jerah went to see him, hoping to learn something that could help him overcome his fear. The old man sat down with Jerah and listened to his concerns. After a while, he spoke:

"Jerah, you have achieved much in this life. But what good is it if you cannot enjoy the fruits of your labor? Your fear of failure has consumed you, and it is time to let it go."

Jerah was taken aback by the old man's words. For so long, he had believed that his fear was what drove him to success. But now, he began to see the truth in the old man's words. He knew that he needed to find a way to overcome his fear if he wanted to live a truly fulfilling life.

Over the following days and weeks, Jerah began to take small steps to overcome his fear. He spent more time with his family and friends, enjoying their company and the simple pleasures of life. He took breaks from his work to admire the beauty of nature and the world around him. And gradually, he began to feel a sense of peace and contentment that he had never experienced before.

As Jerah began to let go of his fear, he found that his business and farming operations continued to thrive. In fact, he was able to achieve even greater success than before, thanks to his newfound sense of calm and focus. But more importantly, Jerah was able to enjoy the fruits of his labor, to appreciate the beauty of the world around him, and to spend time with the people he loved.

As the years went by, Jerah's reputation as a successful

businessman began to fade. But in its place grew a new reputation, one of a man who had overcome his fear and found true happiness and contentment in life.

And when Jerah passed away many years later, the villagers remembered him not for his success, but for the courage he had shown in overcoming his fear and the joy he had brought to those around him. They spoke of him as a true example of what it means to live a fulfilling life and to find peace in the face of fear.

Solitude's Regret: The Tale of Calum, Master Mason of King Solomon's Temple

In the land of Israel, during the reign of King Solomon, the construction of the grand and magnificent Temple for the Lord was underway. The Temple was to be a masterpiece of architecture, a monument to the greatness of God, and a symbol of Israel's prosperity and strength.

Calum, a skilled mason, was one of the workers tasked with building the Temple. Day in and day out, he worked tirelessly to construct the massive structure. With every stone that he laid and every wall that he raised, he put his heart and soul into the project.

Despite his dedication, Calum was a man tormented by demons of depression and isolation. He found himself unable to connect with the other masons and workers on the temple site. Though he worked alongside them for years, he never managed to form any meaningful friendships or bonds.

Calum's struggles with depression and isolation only intensified as the construction of the Temple progressed. He watched as his fellow workers laughed and joked with each other, forming close bonds and enjoying each other's company. But try as he might, he could not seem to break through the barriers that separated him from the others.

As the years passed, the Temple began to take shape. The workers built massive pillars, intricate archways, and elegant courtyards. Calum continued to work tirelessly, pouring his heart and soul into every stone and every brick.

But despite his dedication to the project, Calum was plagued with a sense of regret. He had poured his heart and soul into the temple, but he had neglected to form the connections with his fellow workers that would have made the experience all the more rewarding. He was haunted by thoughts of all the missed opportunities for friendship and camaraderie.

Finally, the day came when the Temple was finished, and King Solomon declared it open for worship. Calum stood in awe, gazing upon the grand structure he had helped to build. The Temple was truly a masterpiece of architecture, a testament to the greatness of God, and a symbol of Israel's strength and prosperity.

But despite the pride he felt in his accomplishment, there was a deep sense of sorrow in his heart. As he looked around at the faces of his fellow workers, he realized that he had missed out on something important. He had been so focused on his work that he had failed to connect with the people around him.

Calum returned to his home village, carrying with him the weight of his regret. For many years, he lived in solitude, haunted by the memories of his time working on the Temple. But as he grew older, he began to understand the importance of forming connections with those around him.

He began to reach out to others, to listen to their stories, and to share his own. Slowly but surely, he began to form meaningful relationships with the people in his village. And though he could never go back in time and change the past, he found a sense of peace and fulfillment in the present.

In the end, Calum came to understand that the true beauty of life lies not in the accomplishments we achieve, but in the relationships we form with the people around us. He may have missed out on the opportunity to bond with his fellow workers while building the Temple, but he would not make the same mistake again. He had learned the value of companionship and the importance of building relationships that would last a lifetime.

Jeduthun's Journey: A Blind Stonecutter's Triumph

Jeduthun was born into a family of stonecutters and was raised in a small village in Israel. As a child, he was fascinated by the intricate designs and shapes his family members were able to create out of stone. He spent most of his childhood watching his father and uncles work and helping them in any way he could.

When Jeduthun turned 14, he decided to follow in his family's footsteps and become a stonecutter himself. His father taught him everything he knew about the craft, and Jeduthun proved to be a quick learner. He had a natural talent for the work, and soon he was able to create beautiful designs of his own.

However, when Jeduthun turned 20, tragedy struck. While working on a building project, a piece of stone fell and hit him in the head, causing him to lose his eyesight. Jeduthun was devastated. He thought that his life was over and that he would never be able to work as a stonecutter again.

Jeduthun's family and friends tried to console him and urged him to find a new profession. But Jeduthun refused to give up on his dream. He was determined to continue working as a stonecutter, even if it meant finding new ways to approach the craft.

Jeduthun spent months in his room, trying to come up with new techniques and approaches that would allow him to continue working. He experimented with different tools and materials and worked tirelessly to perfect his craft.

Eventually, Jeduthun came up with a new approach to stonecutting that relied on his other senses, such as touch and sound. He would feel the stone with his hands and listen to the sound of his chisel hitting the stone to determine the right shape and size.

Jeduthun's new approach to stonecutting was met with skepticism by some of his peers, who believed that a blind person could never create anything of real value. But Jeduthun refused to let their doubts discourage him. He continued to work hard and to refine his technique until he became one of the most sought-after stonecutters in Israel.

Despite his success, Jeduthun never forgot his roots. He continued to work on projects for his village, including a new well and a community center. His work brought great pride to the village, and he became a beloved figure in the community.

One day, Jeduthun received a special commission from the high priest of the temple in Jerusalem. The high priest wanted him to create a new sacred room in the temple, one that would be used for prayer and meditation. Jeduthun was thrilled at the opportunity and eagerly accepted the commission.

Jeduthun spent months working on the sacred room, using his unique approach to stonecutting to create intricate designs and patterns that were both beautiful and functional. He worked tirelessly, day and night, until the room was complete.

When the high priest and other officials saw the sacred room, they were amazed. They had never seen anything like it before.

The room was a testament to Jeduthun's skill and dedication, and it became a symbol of faith and devotion for the entire community.

Jeduthun's journey reminds us that no matter what challenges we face, we can overcome them with perseverance, determination, and hard work. Jeduthun's disability did not limit him; it inspired him to find new ways to approach his craft and to achieve even greater success. He is a true inspiration and a testament to the human spirit.

The Wisdom of Elijah: Learning to Listen and Respect Others

Long ago, in the land of Israel, there lived a wise and respected elder named Elijah. Elijah was not only a skilled master mason but also a man known for his ability to listen to others and offer sound advice. His wisdom and kindness made him a cherished member of the community.

One day, Elijah was approached by a group of young men who were arguing loudly with each other. They were all trying to talk at the same time and no one was listening to what the others had to say. Elijah approached the group and calmly asked, "Why are you all shouting at each other? Why don't you listen to what the others have to say?"

One of the young men replied, "We all have something important to say, and we want to make sure we are heard."

Elijah smiled and replied, "I understand that you all have something important to say, but if everyone talks at the same time, no one will be heard. It's important to listen to others and wait your turn to speak. That way, everyone will have a chance to be heard and understood."

The young men were surprised by Elijah's wise words, but they were also intrigued. They had never considered that waiting their turn to speak could be a sign of respect for others. They began to listen to each other, and Elijah listened to them too.

As the young men began to speak, they realized that they had a lot in common. They shared similar concerns about their community and their families, but they had been so focused on their own thoughts that they had not listened to each other before. Elijah encouraged them to share their thoughts and to listen to each other with an open mind.

The young men took turns speaking, and as they did, they began to understand each other better. They realized that they had all been trying to solve the same problems but had been going about it in different ways. By listening to each other, they were able to come up with a solution that worked for everyone.

From that day on, Elijah's words of wisdom spread throughout the community. People began to respect each other's opinions and to listen to what others had to say. Elijah's legacy of teaching the importance of listening and respecting others lived on for generations to come.

Years later, as Elijah was approaching the end of his life, he was visited by some of the same young men he had counseled many years before. They thanked him for his wisdom and told him how much his words had impacted their lives. They had gone on to become leaders in their community, and they had shared Elijah's message of respect and listening with others.

Elijah smiled, knowing that his legacy would live on long after he was gone. He had taught an important lesson, one that would continue to bring people together and build strong communities.

Rael the Master Mason: Overcoming Frustration to Achieve Dreams

Rael was a master mason, renowned throughout the ancient land of Israel for his skill and craft. He had built some of the most magnificent structures in the kingdom, including palaces, temples, and fortresses.

But despite his many successes, Rael was not immune to frustration. There were times when he would encounter obstacles and setbacks that made him feel like giving up. He knew, however, that to achieve his dreams, he could not let frustration get the better of him.

One day, Rael was approached by a young apprentice who was struggling to carve a stone into the perfect shape. The apprentice had been working on the stone for hours, but no matter how hard he tried, he could not get it right.

Rael watched the young apprentice for a while and then approached him. "Frustration is a natural part of the learning process," he said. "But you must not let it stop you from achieving your dreams."

Rael then took the stone and began to work on it himself. He showed the apprentice how to approach the task from a different angle and with a new perspective. He demonstrated how to take breaks when feeling stuck and how to come back to the task with renewed energy and focus.

Over the course of several hours, Rael and the apprentice worked together, chipping away at the stone until it was finally perfect. The apprentice was amazed at how Rael had been able to overcome the frustration and achieve such a beautiful result.

From that day forward, the young apprentice looked up to Rael not just as a master mason, but also as a wise and patient mentor. Rael had taught him that frustration was normal, but it was possible to overcome it by remaining determined and persistent.

As the years went by, Rael continued to work on his craft, building structures that were more impressive and grander than ever before. But despite his success, Rael never forgot the lessons he had learned about overcoming frustration.

There were many times when Rael faced challenges that seemed insurmountable. Sometimes, his work would be criticized, and he would be told that his designs were impossible to build. But Rael refused to be deterred by these obstacles.

Instead, he would take a step back and think about the problem from a different perspective. He would brainstorm new ideas and approaches, always pushing himself to think creatively and outside the box.

And with each challenge he faced, Rael emerged stronger and more determined than ever before. He knew that frustration was just a temporary setback, and that with hard work and persistence, he could achieve anything he set his mind to.

Years later, when Rael was an old man, the young apprentice who he had helped so many years before became a master mason in his own right. He remembered the lessons that Rael had taught him and passed them on to the next generation of apprentices.

And so, Rael's legacy lived on, not just in the magnificent structures he had built, but in the hearts and minds of those he had inspired to overcome frustration and achieve their dreams. Rael had taught them that no matter how difficult a task may seem, with persistence and determination, anything is possible.

Learning Through Mistakes: The Story of Nael the Apprentice Mason

Nael was an apprentice mason who lived in a small village on the outskirts of a great city. From a young age, he had always been fascinated by the structures that surrounded him, from the towering walls of the city to the majestic temples that dotted the landscape. He dreamed of one day creating buildings that would stand the test of time, just like those he admired.

When he was old enough, Nael began to study under a skilled stonemason, who was known throughout the city for his talent and craftsmanship. At first, Nael was intimidated by his master's skill, but he was also eager to learn everything he could from him.

In the beginning, Nael's tasks were simple, such as fetching water and carrying stones. However, as he gained more experience, his master began to entrust him with more challenging tasks, such as chiseling stones and laying bricks.

Nael took his work seriously, and he worked diligently to master each new skill his master taught him. However, no matter how hard he tried, he still made mistakes. Sometimes his hand would slip while chiseling, or he would lay a brick crookedly. Each time he did, his master would remind him that making mistakes was a natural part of the learning process and that as long as he kept trying and learning from his mistakes, he would eventually become a skilled craftsman.

At first, Nael felt ashamed of his mistakes, worrying that they made him a failure in his master's eyes. But as he continued to work and learn, he began to understand the importance of making mistakes. Each time he made a mistake, he would take a deep breath, correct his error, and move forward with renewed determination. Slowly but surely, he began to see his skills as a mason grow.

As the years passed, Nael worked on many projects with his master, from small homes to grand temples. He continued to learn new skills and techniques, and he always kept his master's advice in mind: that making mistakes was natural, and that the key to success was to keep trying and learning from them.

One day, Nael was given the task of carving intricate designs into the walls of a temple. It was a challenging task, and Nael worked for hours on end, carefully chiseling away at the stone until the design was perfect. However, just as he was finishing the final touches, his hand slipped, and he made a mistake.

Nael was devastated. He had put so much effort into the design, and now it was ruined. His master noticed his distress and comforted him, telling him once again that making mistakes was natural and that he should not give up. Instead, he should correct his mistake and keep trying.

With his master's encouragement, Nael took a deep breath and began to correct his error. Slowly but surely, he chiseled away at the stone, working carefully until the design was perfect once again.

When the temple was finally completed, the high priest came to inspect the work. He examined the intricate designs on the walls and stopped at one section, which was particularly impressive.

"Who carved this section?" the high priest asked.

"Nael did, your grace," his master replied.

"Nael, you have done a wonderful job. Your attention to detail is truly remarkable," the high priest praised.

Nael beamed with pride, knowing that all of his hard work and determination had paid off. He had learned that making mistakes was natural, and that the key to success was to keep trying and learning from them.

As he looked back on his journey, Nael realized that his mistakes had been his greatest teachers. They had pushed him to work harder, think more carefully, and ultimately become the skilled mason he had always dreamed

The Mason's Trials: A Tale of Job's Perseverance and Understanding

Once upon a time, in a small village nestled in the rolling hills of the Israel, there lived a young apprentice mason named Job. He had grown up in the village, learning the craft of building and construction from his father. He had always been known as a hard worker, eager to learn and improve his skills.

But Job's life was about to take a turn for the worse. One day, his village was raided by a band of marauders. They burned down homes, stole livestock, and killed many of the villagers. Job was lucky to escape with his life, but he lost everything else. His home, his tools, and all of his possessions were gone in a matter of hours.

Feeling lost and alone, Job set out to find a new place to call home. He wandered for many days, trying to find work as a mason to support himself. But everywhere he went, he was turned away. People were suspicious of him, thinking he might be a spy for the marauders who had attacked their village. Job felt discouraged, but he refused to give up.

Finally, Job arrived in a new village. The people there were hesitant to trust him, but he was able to prove his worth as a mason. He began to build homes and walls, earning a small income that helped him to survive. Over time, the people of the village began to accept Job as one of their own.

But Job's troubles were far from over. One day, he fell ill with a mysterious illness that left him bedridden for weeks. He was unable to work and soon found himself in dire straits. He had no money for medicine or food, and he felt as though he was on the brink of death.

In his darkest hour, Job began to question why he had been subjected to such trials. Had he done something to deserve this fate? Was he being punished for something he had done in the past?

But then, Job began to realize something important. Through all of his trials and tribulations, he had gained a new perspective on life. He had learned to empathize with others who had suffered similar hardships. He had discovered that there was more to people than meets the eye, and that it was important to try to truly understand what someone else's life was like.

With this newfound understanding, Job began to recover. He slowly regained his strength and his masonry skills, and he continued to build and create. He became known throughout the village as a wise and compassionate man, someone who had faced incredible trials but had emerged stronger for it.

And so, Job's story serves as a reminder to all of us that life is full of trials and tribulations. But through perseverance and understanding, we can emerge from these trials as stronger and wiser individuals.

The Empathy of Hiral: An Old Testament Tale of a Mason's Apprentice

In the bustling city of Jerusalem, Hiral worked as an apprentice mason under the guidance of his master. He had always been fascinated by the art of stone-cutting and building, and he had worked hard to learn the techniques and skills needed to become a master mason himself one day.

Hiral's master was known throughout the city for his exquisite craftsmanship and attention to detail. He had built some of the most beautiful and impressive buildings in Jerusalem, including the temple that stood at the heart of the city.

Under his master's guidance, Hiral had learned to take great pride in his work. He would spend long hours chiseling and shaping stones to perfection, and his work was admired by all who saw it.

One day, as Hiral was working on a particularly challenging piece of stone, he overheard a conversation between two men. They were discussing the poor living conditions of the city's less fortunate, who lived in shoddy huts and struggled to make ends meet.

Hiral felt a pang of empathy for these people he had never met, and he wondered what it must be like to live in such conditions. He tried to imagine himself in their shoes, and he felt a deep sense of sadness.

As he continued to work, Hiral couldn't shake the feeling that he needed to do something to help. He decided to speak to his master about his concerns, hoping that together they could find a way to make a difference.

To his surprise, his master was already well aware of the plight of the poor in Jerusalem. He had been working with a group of builders to construct affordable housing for the less fortunate, but they had encountered a problem. They didn't have enough skilled workers to help with the project.

Hiral's master saw this as an opportunity to not only help those in need but also to teach his apprentice a valuable lesson in empathy. He asked Hiral to join the team of builders and use his skills to help build the homes for the poor.

Hiral eagerly accepted the challenge and threw himself into the project with all his heart. As he worked side by side with the other builders, he began to understand the struggles and challenges they faced every day.

He saw firsthand how hard they worked to provide for their families and realized that they were not so different from himself. He felt a deep sense of empathy for their struggles, and he worked even harder to ensure that the homes they were building were of the highest quality.

Despite the long hours and hard work, Hiral found great joy in helping to build homes for the less fortunate. He saw the gratitude in the faces of the people who would soon call these houses their homes, and he felt a sense of fulfillment that he had never experienced before.

As the project neared completion, Hiral felt a sense of pride and satisfaction that he had never felt before. He knew that he had made a difference in the lives of the poor, and he had learned a valuable lesson in empathy.

From that day on, Hiral made a vow to always put himself in someone else's shoes and to try to understand their struggles and challenges. He knew that this was the only way to truly make a difference in the world and to build a better future for all.

Years later, when Hiral had become a master mason himself, he would tell the story of his apprenticeship and the lesson he learned about empathy. He would remind others that the key to building a better world was not just in the quality of the buildings they constructed, but in the compassion and understanding they showed towards their fellow human beings.

Master Mason Eli: Learning the Pain of Exclusion and the Power of Inclusion

Master Mason Eli had been working on King Solomon's temple for several years now. His skills were renowned throughout Jerusalem, and he was highly respected by his colleagues for his exceptional craftsmanship. Despite his many years of experience, he still relished the opportunity to work on such a significant project, and every day he put all his effort into building a temple that would be the envy of the world.

As the work progressed, however, Eli began to feel left out. He noticed that many of his coworkers had formed close-knit groups, and they often excluded him from their conversations and activities. He tried to join in, but he found himself on the sidelines more often than not. It seemed that no matter how hard he tried, he could not shake off the feeling of loneliness and isolation that had begun to take root in his heart.

One day, while taking a break from his work, Eli sat down under a tree and began to reflect on his situation. He realized that he had been so focused on his work that he had forgotten to reach out to others and make an effort to connect with them. He had become so consumed with the construction of the temple that he had neglected the human element of his work.

Determined to make a change, Eli decided to take the initiative and reach out to those who had previously excluded him. He started small, by offering to help one of his coworkers with a particularly difficult task. To his surprise, his gesture was warmly received, and he was invited to join in their conversation during their break. As he continued to make an effort to connect with others, he found that he was no longer alone and felt a sense of belonging among his coworkers.

Over time, Eli's efforts to connect with his coworkers began to bear fruit. He found himself invited to more and more gatherings, and his colleagues started to see him as a valuable member of their team. He learned about their families, their interests, and their hopes for the future. They, in turn, began to appreciate him for his skills and experience, and they began to seek out his opinion on the finer points of the temple's construction.

Eli had learned a valuable lesson that it hurts to be left out, but the power of inclusion is a force that can bring people together. He had come to realize that building the temple was not just about laying bricks and chiseling stones; it was about building relationships with his fellow workers. As he continued to reach out to those who were excluded, he found that the temple was not just a physical structure but also a symbol of the unity that can be achieved when people work together towards a common goal.

Years passed, and the temple was now completed. It was a masterpiece of excellence that would stand the test of time, a testament to the skill and dedication of those who had built it. But for Eli, the true legacy of the temple was not the physical structure but the relationships he had formed with his coworkers. As he looked back on his time working on the temple, he realized that the lessons he had learned about the power of inclusion were just as important as his skills as a master mason.

The Stonecutter's Second Chance: How Jonah Learned to Look for the Good in Life

Jonah had been a master mason for as long as he could remember. He had spent most of his life working with stone, creating beautiful sculptures and buildings that were admired by all who saw them. His reputation as a skilled craftsman had spread throughout the land, and he was highly sought after by those who wanted the best stonework done.

Despite his success, Jonah was not a happy man. He had a tendency to dwell on the negative aspects of his life, and he was never satisfied with what he had. He was always looking for more, always striving for something better, and never really taking the time to appreciate what he already had.

One day, Jonah was working on a project for a wealthy merchant. He was carving a beautiful statue out of a block of marble, and he was completely absorbed in his work. But as he was chipping away at the stone, his chisel slipped and he made a mistake. The statue was ruined.

Jonah was beside himself with anger and frustration. He cursed and shouted, and he threw his chisel down on the ground. He was about to give up on the project altogether when a voice spoke to him.

"Jonah, why are you so upset?" asked the voice.

Jonah looked around, but he couldn't see anyone. "Who's there?" he asked.

"It's me, God," said the voice. "I've been watching you for a long time, Jonah. I've seen how you focus on the bad things in life, and how you never seem to appreciate the good."

Jonah was surprised. He had always believed in God, but he had never thought that God would speak to him directly. "What do you want me to do?" he asked.

"I want you to learn to look for the good in life," said God. "I want you to see that even when things go wrong, there is always something to be grateful for."

Jonah wasn't sure how to do that, but he decided to try. He picked up his chisel and started working on the statue again. This time, he tried to focus on the beauty of the marble and the joy of creating something new. He tried to let go of his anger and frustration and to look for the good in the situation.

As he worked, Jonah began to feel a sense of peace and contentment that he had never experienced before. He started to notice the beauty in the world around him, and he began to appreciate the good things in his life. He realized that he had been so focused on the bad things that he had missed all the good things that were right in front of him.

Jonah started to see the world in a different way. He realized that every day was a gift, and that even when things didn't go his way, there was always something to be grateful for. He began to take the time to appreciate the beauty of nature, the kindness of strangers, and the love of his family and friends.

In the end, Jonah finished the statue, and it was more beautiful than anything he had ever created before. But more importantly, he had learned a valuable lesson. He had learned that it's important to look for the good in life, even when things go wrong. He had learned that gratitude and appreciation can bring peace and happiness, even in the midst of difficult times. And he had learned that sometimes, a second chance is all you need to find your way back to the good.

From that day forward, Jonah lived his life with a new perspective. He was no longer focused on the negative aspects of his life. Instead, he looked for the good in everything, and he found that his life was filled with joy and happiness. He continued to create beautiful sculptures and buildings, but he did it with a sense of joy and gratitude that he had never felt before. His work became even more magnificent because he was now able to see the beauty in every piece of stone he worked with.

People began to notice a change in Jonah. He was no longer grumpy or irritable. Instead, he was always smiling and eager to help others. He became known for his kindness and generosity, and people sought him out not only for his skills as a mason but also for his wise counsel and comforting presence.

One day, a young apprentice came to Jonah for advice. The young man had made a mistake while working on a project, and he was devastated. He felt that he had ruined everything and that he would never be able to make it right.

Jonah listened patiently to the young man's story, and he could see the despair in his eyes. But instead of scolding him or criticizing him, Jonah shared his own story of how he had learned to look for the good in life.

He told the young man about his own mistake with the marble statue, and how he had almost given up on it. But he had decided to try again, to look for the beauty in the stone, and to appreciate the joy of creating something new.

"Life is like that, my young friend," Jonah said. "Sometimes we make mistakes, and sometimes things don't go as planned. But it's how we respond to those challenges that makes all the difference. If we focus on the bad, we will only see more bad. But if we look for the good, we will find it, even in the darkest of times."

The young apprentice listened intently, and Jonah could see the spark of hope in his eyes. "Thank you, master," the young man said. "I will try to remember your words and to look for the good in every situation."

And with that, the young man went back to his work, determined to do his best and to find the good in every stone he worked with.

As for Jonah, he continued to live his life with a sense of gratitude and appreciation for all the good things in his life. He knew that he had been given a second chance to see the world in a new way, and he was determined to make the most of it.

And so, the story of Jonah, the stone cutter who learned to look for the good in life, became a legend. People told the story for generations, passing down the wisdom of the old master mason to each new generation. And in every retelling of the story, people were reminded of the power of gratitude and the importance of looking for the good in every situation.

Aeli's Lesson of Gratitude

In the small town of Nazareth, nestled in the hills of ancient Israel, there lived a young man named Aeli. Aeli was an apprentice mason, working hard every day to learn the trade of stone-cutting and building. He spent his days chiseling and shaping blocks of stone, carefully fitting them together to create sturdy walls and grand structures.

Aeli was a diligent and hardworking apprentice, but he often felt tired and discouraged. He would look around at the world and see so much pain, suffering, and hardship. He wondered how he could find joy and gratitude in a world filled with so much sorrow.

One day, Aeli's master mason called him over to a new project. They were building a temple in honor of their God, and it was going to be a grand structure indeed. Aeli was thrilled to be a part of such an important project.

As he worked on the temple, Aeli began to notice something remarkable. Each stone he lifted, each block he cut, was a testament to the many blessings in his life. He had a steady job, a roof over his head, food on the table, and a community of friends and family who supported him.

Aeli began to see that he had so many wonderful reasons to be thankful in his life every day. He started to feel a deep sense of gratitude for everything he had, no matter how small or seemingly insignificant.

One day, as he was carving a block of stone, Aeli overheard a group of people nearby. They were talking about a terrible famine that was sweeping across the land. Many people were going hungry, and there was little food to be found.

Aeli felt a pang of sadness and compassion for those who were suffering. But he also felt a renewed sense of gratitude for the blessings in his own life. He realized that even in the midst of pain and hardship, there were always reasons to be grateful.

As he finished his work on the temple, Aeli felt a deep sense of satisfaction and pride. He had learned an important lesson about gratitude, and he knew that it would stay with him for the rest of his life.

Years went by, and Aeli became a master mason himself. He built many grand structures and continued to teach others the trade. But no matter where he went or what he did, he never forgot the lesson he had learned on that temple construction site. He always remembered to find reasons to be grateful, even in the darkest of times.

As Aeli grew older, he became known throughout the land as a wise and respected elder. People would come to him seeking advice and guidance, and he would always share the story of his lesson of gratitude.

One day, a young boy came to Aeli with a heavy heart. He had lost his parents to illness, and he felt lost and alone in the world. Aeli listened to the boy's story with compassion and understanding.

Then, he told the boy the story of his lesson of gratitude. He talked about the many blessings in his life, and how they had helped him find joy and contentment even in difficult times. He encouraged the boy to look for reasons to be grateful, even in the midst of his pain and loss.

The boy listened to Aeli's words, and something shifted inside him. He began to see that even in the midst of his sorrow, there were still things to be thankful for. He felt a sense of hope and peace that he hadn't felt in a long time.

From that day on, the boy would visit Aeli often, and they would talk about gratitude and the many blessings in their lives. Aeli was grateful for the opportunity to pass on his lesson of gratitude to the next generation.

And so, the story of Aeli's Lesson of Gratitude was passed down from generation to generation, becoming a beloved tale of wisdom and inspiration throughout the land.

As the years went by, Aeli grew old and eventually passed away. But his legacy lived on in the hearts and minds of those he had touched with his lesson of gratitude.

The temple that Aeli had helped build stood strong and majestic, a testament to the hard work and dedication of its builders. But it also stood as a symbol of something deeper, a reminder that even in the midst of difficult times, there are always reasons to be grateful.

As people walked past the temple, they would often pause and reflect on the story of Aeli's Lesson of Gratitude. They would remember the wise old mason who had taught them to look for the blessings in their lives, no matter how small or seemingly insignificant.

And so, the lesson of gratitude continued to be passed down from generation to generation, reminding people of the power of gratitude to transform even the darkest of times into something beautiful and meaningful. And for that, they were forever grateful.

The Stone Mason's Stewardship

John was a skilled master mason living in a small village nestled in the hills. His reputation for creating sturdy structures that lasted for generations had spread far and wide, and he was well respected by his peers and customers alike.

John had always been fascinated by the natural world around him. He marveled at the beauty of the trees and flowers, the song of the birds, and the playful antics of the forest creatures. Despite his busy schedule, John would often take a walk in the forest to clear his mind and reconnect with nature.

One day, while taking a stroll, John discovered a beautiful clearing filled with lush greenery and colorful wildflowers. However, as he looked closer, he saw that the clearing was littered with trash and debris. This saddened John, and he knew that something had to be done.

He decided to take it upon himself to clean up the clearing. He spent many hours gathering the trash and debris, separating recyclable materials, and digging holes to bury the waste properly. As he worked, he noticed the animals of the forest watching him with curiosity. The birds perched on nearby branches and chirped their approval, and even the squirrels and rabbits came out of hiding to help.

Over the next few days, John continued to work on the clearing, making it more beautiful with each passing moment. He planted new trees and flowers, and he even built a small bench for people to sit and enjoy the scenery.

As he sat on the bench, taking in the beauty of his work, John felt a sense of pride and joy. But he also felt a sense of responsibility. He knew that the world was a precious place, and it was up to each of us to care for it and protect it.

From that day forward, John made it his mission to teach others about the importance of stewardship and caring for the world around us. He shared his knowledge with other masons, and he even traveled to nearby villages to spread his message.

John's teachings were so powerful that they inspired many people to take action and care for the world around them. He encouraged people to recycle, to plant trees, and to conserve resources. He taught them that even small actions could make a big difference in protecting the earth.

Years went by, and John grew old. His hands became stiff, and his legs grew tired, but his spirit remained strong. Even in his old age, he continued to spread his message of stewardship and encourage others to care for the world.

When John finally passed away, the villagers mourned his loss but celebrated his legacy. They named the clearing where he had worked "John's Meadow" and dedicated it to his memory. They continued to care for the meadow, planting new trees and flowers and picking up any litter that might have been left behind.

As time passed, John's message of stewardship continued to spread, inspiring new generations to care for the world around them.

The Ripple Effect: The Story of Elih, the Apprentice Mason

Elih was a young man who had grown up in a family of master builders. From a young age, he had been fascinated by the craft of masonry, watching in awe as his father and grandfather worked tirelessly to create beautiful structures that stood the test of time.

When Elih was old enough, he became an apprentice to his father, eager to learn everything there was to know about the trade. He spent his days chipping away at stone, shaping it with his hammer and chisel until it fit perfectly into place. He learned to mix mortar and lay bricks, and he even helped design some of the more intricate patterns and shapes that his father created.

Despite his love for his craft, Elih often felt like his work was insignificant. He was just one small part of a much larger project, and it seemed like his individual actions didn't really matter all that much in the grand scheme of things.

One day, as Elih was walking through the town square, he saw a group of children playing by the fountain. They were throwing pebbles into the water, watching as the ripples spread out in ever-widening circles.

As he watched the children play, Elih had a sudden realization: just like the pebbles in the fountain, our actions have a ripple effect that extends far beyond ourselves. Every small action we take, no matter how insignificant it may seem, can have a profound impact on the world around us.

From that day forward, Elih approached his work with a new sense of purpose. He realized that every stone he laid, every brick he placed, every drop of mortar he mixed - it all mattered. His work was a small but crucial piece of a much larger puzzle, and he took pride in knowing that his efforts were helping to create something truly beautiful.

Over time, Elih's skills as a mason grew. He learned to work with a wide variety of materials, from stone and brick to wood and metal. He honed his abilities to design and create complex structures that were not only beautiful but also practical and functional.

But even as his skill grew, Elih never forgot the lesson of the ripple effect. He knew that every small action he took, no matter how seemingly insignificant, could have a profound impact on the world around him.

One day, as Elih was working on a particularly challenging project, he encountered a young apprentice named Samuel. Like Elih, Samuel was just starting out in the world of masonry, and he was struggling to keep up with the demands of the job.

Elih saw something of himself in the young apprentice, and he took Samuel under his wing, teaching him everything he knew about the craft of masonry. He showed him how to shape stone, how to lay brick, and how to mix mortar.

But perhaps most importantly, Elih taught Samuel about the power of the ripple effect. He explained to him that every small action he took, every stone he shaped, every brick he laid - it all mattered. And he encouraged Samuel to approach his work with the same sense of purpose and dedication that he himself had learned to embrace.

Years later, long after Elih had become a master mason in his own right, he was walking through the town square once again. This time, he saw a group of apprentices hard at work, shaping stones and laying bricks just as he had done so many years before.

Elih approached the young apprentices and offered them a piece of advice that he had learned through his own experience: "Remember that every stone you lay, every brick you place, every drop of mortar you mix - it all matters. Your actions may seem small, but they have the power to create ripples that will spread far beyond yourself."

And with that, Elih continued on his way, knowing that he had passed on an important lesson to the next generation of masons. He felt a sense of pride in knowing that his work had not only created beautiful structures but had also helped to shape the lives and careers of countless apprentices who would go on to make their own contributions to the world.

As Elih walked away from the town square, he couldn't help but reflect on the power of the ripple effect. He knew that his actions, no matter how small, had contributed to something much greater than himself. And he realized that the same was true for all of us - every action we take, no matter how seemingly insignificant, has the potential to create a ripple effect that can shape the world in ways we may never fully realize.

From that day forward, Elih continued to approach his work and his life with a newfound sense of purpose and dedication. He knew that his actions mattered, and he was determined to make every one count. And he hoped that others would learn from his example, embracing the power of the ripple effect and using it to create positive change in their own lives and in the world around them.

Eriah the Master Mason: A Lesson in Honesty and Integrity

Eriah was a highly skilled and respected master mason in ancient Israel. His work was known far and wide, and he had earned the reputation of being the best in his field. He had been involved in many construction projects, from building houses and bridges to designing and constructing temples.

One day, the king summoned Eriah to his palace and presented him with a challenging task. The king wanted to build a grand temple in honor of their god, and he wanted Eriah to design and construct the entire structure. The king was eager to see his vision come to life and demanded that Eriah complete the project within a year.

Eriah was thrilled to receive such an honor and immediately began working on the plans. He knew that this was the most important project he had ever undertaken and that he needed to give it his all. However, as he worked on the design, he realized that the plan he had in mind would take longer than a year to complete.

He knew that the temple's construction required intricate details and high-quality materials, which would take time to procure. Additionally, the construction work would be extensive and required careful attention to detail. Eriah knew that if he told the king the truth, it would disappoint him, and he would risk losing the king's favor.

Eriah could have taken shortcuts to complete the temple within the year, but he knew that this would compromise the quality of the building. Eriah had always believed that honesty was the best policy, even if it meant disappointing someone. He knew that if he agreed to the king's deadline, the temple would not be as impressive as it should be. Eriah was in a quandary, knowing that he needed to keep the king happy while also ensuring the temple's quality.

After much contemplation, Eriah decided to approach the king and explain the situation to him. He told the king that while he could complete the temple within a year, it would require shortcuts that would compromise the quality of the building. Eriah explained that if the king was willing to extend the deadline, he could ensure that the temple was built to the highest standards.

The king was initially disappointed by Eriah's honesty. He had hoped that the temple would be completed within a year and didn't want to wait any longer. But eventually, he realized that Eriah's integrity was more important than his desire for a quick completion. The king agreed to Eriah's request and extended the deadline.

Eriah worked tirelessly on the temple for three years, ensuring that every detail was perfect. He sourced the best materials and hired the best craftsmen to assist him in the work. Eriah knew that this was his most significant project and that it had to be completed to perfection. He had a reputation to uphold, and he was determined to ensure that the temple would be a testament to his skill and dedication.

The king was amazed by the final result and praised Eriah's work. The temple was the most impressive building that had ever been constructed in the kingdom. The king thanked Eriah for his honesty and integrity, and from that day forward, Eriah was the king's most trusted advisor and friend.

Eriah's honesty and integrity had won him the respect and admiration of the king and the people. He had demonstrated that even when it was difficult, it was important to be honest and to do the right thing. Eriah's story serves as a reminder to us all that honesty and integrity are essential virtues and that they are the foundation of lasting success and respect.

The Conscience of the Mason

In the ancient city of Jerusalem, there lived a young man named Aaron who was an apprentice mason. Aaron was a dedicated worker, and he was known throughout the city for his skill and his attention to detail. But what truly set him apart from his peers was his unwavering sense of honesty and accountability.

Aaron had been taught from a young age that it was always better to own up to one's mistakes, no matter how difficult it might be. He had seen firsthand the damage that could be caused by deceit and dishonesty, and he was determined to live his life with integrity and honor.

One day, the master mason tasked Aaron with building a wall around the city. It was a massive project, and Aaron knew that he would have to work hard and be diligent if he wanted to succeed. But he was up for the challenge, and he set to work with a sense of purpose and determination.

As the days went by, the wall began to take shape. Aaron worked tirelessly, laying brick after brick with precision and care. His fellow apprentices marveled at his skill, and the people of Jerusalem watched in awe as the wall grew taller and stronger with each passing day.

But one morning, the master mason discovered that a section of the wall was flawed. The bricks were crooked and uneven, and it was clear that the person responsible had tried to cover up their mistake.

The master mason was furious. He called all of his apprentices together and demanded to know who was responsible for the flawed section of the wall. Aaron felt a knot form in his stomach as he realized that he was the one who had made the mistake. He had been rushing to finish his work, and in his haste, he had neglected to properly align the bricks.

For a moment, Aaron considered keeping quiet. He knew that admitting his mistake would mean facing the wrath of the master mason, and he feared that he might lose his apprenticeship altogether. But then he remembered the lessons of his youth, and he knew that he could not live with himself if he did not own up to what he had done.

With a deep breath, Aaron stepped forward and confessed to the master mason that he had made the mistake. The other apprentices looked on in shock as the master mason berated Aaron for his carelessness. But Aaron did not flinch. He knew that he had done the right thing, and he stood before the master mason with his head held high.

As the days went by, the other apprentices began to see Aaron in a new light. They had always respected him for his skill, but now they looked up to him for his honesty and integrity. They realized that Aaron was more than just a skilled mason - he was a role model, a beacon of hope in a world that often seemed dark and uncertain.

And as for the flawed section of the wall, Aaron worked tirelessly to fix his mistake. He spent long hours carefully removing the crooked bricks and replacing them with new ones. It was a difficult and time-consuming task, but Aaron knew that it was the only way to make things right. In the end, the wall was stronger and more beautiful than ever before. And Aaron was respected and admired throughout the city for his sense of accountability and his unwavering commitment to honesty and integrity.

Aaron's example reminds us that owning up to our mistakes is not always easy, but it is always the right thing to do. It takes courage and strength to admit when we have done wrong, but it is only through this admission that we can learn and grow. And when we do, we can become like Aaron - beacons of hope in a world that often seems dark and uncertain.

Erza's Lesson on Brotherhood

In the land of Canaan, there lived a young man named Erza, who had always been fascinated by the art of stonemasonry. He had watched his father work as a mason since he was a young boy and had always dreamed of following in his footsteps. When Erza was old enough, he began to work as an apprentice under a master craftsman named Jacob.

Jacob was a stern but fair teacher who demanded nothing less than perfection from his apprentices. Erza was a diligent worker, always striving to improve his skills and impress his master. But despite his efforts, he found it difficult to get along with his fellow apprentices. They were constantly competing with one another, each one trying to outdo the others in the eyes of the master.

Erza found this constant competition exhausting, and he often felt lonely and isolated. He longed for companionship, for the sense of camaraderie that he had seen among other craftsmen. But no matter how hard he tried to fit in with the other apprentices, he always felt like an outsider.

One day, as Erza was working on a project with his fellow apprentices, he accidentally dropped a heavy stone on his foot. He cried out in pain and was unable to continue working. His fellow apprentices, instead of helping him, laughed at his misfortune and mocked him. Erza felt hurt and alone, and he began to wonder if he would ever find true companionship.

Feeling dejected, Erza decided to take a walk and clear his

mind. As he walked, he came across a group of shepherds who were tending their flocks. The shepherds welcomed Erza and offered him food and drink, even though he was a stranger to them. As they ate and drank together, Erza began to feel a sense of camaraderie and brotherhood that he had never experienced before.

As the day went on, Erza spent time with the shepherds, learning about their way of life and listening to their stories. He discovered that they were a tightly-knit community, bound together by a sense of mutual support and shared values. Even though they came from different backgrounds and had different beliefs, they treated each other with kindness and respect.

Erza was deeply moved by this experience, and he realized that he had been missing out on something important in his life. He returned to the mason's workshop with a newfound appreciation for brotherhood and a determination to treat his fellow apprentices with the same kindness and respect he had seen in the shepherds.

From that day on, Erza worked hard to build positive relationships with his fellow apprentices. He took the time to get to know them as individuals, and he made a conscious effort to show them kindness and support. Slowly but surely, the other apprentices began to respond in kind, and Erza found that he was no longer alone. He had become part of a community, bound together by a sense of brotherhood and mutual respect.

As Erza completed his apprenticeship and became a master mason in his own right, he never forgot the lessons he had learned from the shepherds. He continued to treat his fellow workers with kindness and respect, and he instilled these values in the apprentices he took on himself. And in this way, Erza's lesson on brotherhood lived on, passed down from one generation of craftsmen to the next, a testament to the power of love and community in a world that so often feels cold and lonely.

Erza's journey towards understanding the importance of brotherhood was not an easy one. In fact, it was filled with many obstacles and challenges along the way. But through it all, Erza remained determined to learn and grow, to become the best version of himself that he could be. And through his perseverance and dedication, Erza not only became a skilled mason, but also a respected leader in his community.

As Erza's reputation grew, people from all over the land came to him seeking his expertise and guidance. Erza welcomed them all with open arms, never turning away anyone in need. He treated everyone with the same kindness and respect, whether they were rich or poor, powerful or powerless.

Through his example, Erza showed others the power of brotherhood and the importance of treating all people with love and compassion. He became a beacon of hope and a symbol of unity in a world that was often torn apart by conflict and division.

Years passed, and Erza grew old and eventually passed away. But his legacy lived on, passed down from one generation to the next. The apprentices that he had taught went on to become master craftsmen themselves, passing on his lessons of brotherhood and compassion to their own apprentices.

And so it went, down through the ages, a never-ending chain of love and brotherhood that stretched across the generations. Erza's lesson had become a part of the fabric of their society, a reminder of the power of unity and the importance of loving thy neighbor.

In the end, Erza's life was a testament to the enduring power of love and brotherhood, a reminder that even in the darkest of times, there is always hope. And though he may have been just one man, he had touched the lives of countless others, leaving a lasting impact that would be felt for generations to come.

The Mason's Mercy: A Tale of Jeau and the Forgotten

In the small village of Aras, nestled between the rolling hills of a great kingdom, there lived a master mason named Jeau. Jeau was renowned for his exceptional craftsmanship and his ability to build towering structures that seemed to touch the sky. He had been a builder for over 50 years and had worked on many grand projects, including the castle of the king himself.

Jeau was a humble man who valued hard work, honesty, and most of all, kindness. Despite his many accomplishments, he always remained true to himself and never lost sight of what was truly important. He believed that the purpose of his craft was not just to create impressive structures, but to help those less fortunate and make a positive impact on the world.

One day, as Jeau was walking through the village square, he noticed a group of beggars huddled together, shivering in the cold. Their ragged clothing barely kept them warm, and their faces were haggard and gaunt from hunger. Jeau was moved by their plight and knew he had to do something to help them.

He invited the beggars to his workshop and gave them food and drink. He listened to their stories and learned that they had been forgotten by the people of the kingdom. They had no family, no home, and no means to support themselves. Jeau was saddened by their plight and vowed to do whatever he could to help them.

Over the next few weeks, Jeau spent all his free time building a shelter for the beggars. He used his expertise as a master mason to create a sturdy structure that would protect them from the harsh elements. He also taught them how to build their own shelter and provided them with the tools and materials they needed to do so.

Jeau did not stop there. He also provided the beggars with food, clothing, and medicine. He even found them work as laborers in the village, so they could earn a living and regain their dignity. Jeau believed that everyone deserved a chance to live with respect and dignity, and he worked tirelessly to make this a reality for the beggars.

The people of the village were amazed by Jeau's kindness and generosity. They had never seen anyone care so much for the less fortunate. Word of Jeau's good deeds spread throughout the kingdom, and soon people from all over were coming to see the shelter he had built and to learn from his example.

Jeau's act of kindness had a ripple effect, and soon others began to follow in his footsteps. The forgotten people of the kingdom were no longer ignored or shunned, but were treated with respect and kindness. They were given jobs, food, and shelter, and were no longer forced to live in the shadows of society.

Years passed, and Jeau grew old. His body was weak, but his spirit remained strong. He knew that his time on earth was coming to an end, but he was at peace knowing that he had made a difference in the lives of so many.

As Jeau lay on his deathbed, the beggars he had helped gathered around him. They held his hand and prayed for his soul. They knew that without his kindness, they would have remained forgotten, but because of him, they had found hope and a new life.

From that day on, the shelter that Jeau had built became a symbol of kindness and compassion. It stood as a reminder to all that no matter how great our skills or accomplishments, it is our acts of kindness that truly define us. Jeau's legacy lived on, and the people of the kingdom continued to honor his memory by caring for the less fortunate and building a better world for all.

www.ingramcontent.com/pod-product-compliance
Lightning Source LLC
Chambersburg PA
CBHW051048250726
48656CB00001B/210